PreK-1

BAGS

How to Use Paper and Plastic Bags to Make Activities
(that meet state standards)
for Your Classroom

by Sharon MacDonald

Grasshopper Press
15215 Chalet Drive
San Antonio, Texas

This book is dedicated (in almost alphabetical order) to Alex, Babbs, Kesey, Princess, Tracy, and Youduh...and in remembrance to Anthony, Camouflage, Charlie the turtle, Checkbook, Fish, Flower, Mercedes, Muffin, Rough, Snowball, Stanley, Waffle, and Perseval, the rooster-chicken.

Pets know the value of bags.

The entire contents Copyright © 2003 by Grasshopper Press. However, the individual purchaser of this book may reproduce materials for classroom and individual use. The purchase of this book may not reproduce any part for an entire school, a school district, or a school system.

Editor: G.T. Nave
Illustrations: Sharon MacDonald

<u>Disclaimer</u>
The publisher and the author cannot be held responsible for damages, mishap, or injury resulting from the use of these activities or because they are presented in this form to the reader. The author recommends appropriate and reasonable supervision at all times based upon the age, ability, physical development, and the intellectual capacity of each child.

ISBN 0-9705949-3-3

Table of Contents

Introduction 1
Activities in Bags
    1. Puppets 3
    2. Storyboards 6
    3. Story-Tag Bag 8
    4. Masks 10
    5. Story-Telling Bag 13
    6. Lunch-Bag Diary 13
    7. Stick Puppets On Stage 16
    8. Tri-Level Book 18
    9. Rhyming Bags 21
    10. Topic-Word Bag 22
    11. Environmental-Print Reading Bag 23
    12. Creative Writing Bag 24
    13. Baggie Books 25
    14. Lunch-Bag Tree 26
    15. Sequence-Board Bag 27
    16. What's in the Bag? 28
    17. Checkerboard Bag 30
    18. Paper-Bag Kite 30
    19. Paper-Bag Flower Pot 33
    20. All-About-Me Box 34
    21. Ice Cream in a Baggie 37
    22. Puzzle Bag 39
    23. "What Am I?" 41
    24. Questions and Answer (Q&A) Bag 42
    25. Paper-Bag "Buildings" 43
    26. Paper-Bag Streamer 44
    27. Art Display Bags 45
    28. Clean Up Bags 46
    29. Cares and Troubles in a Bag 47
    30. Toy Totes 47

Centers in Bags
- 1. Working-with-Words Center 52
- 2. Spelling Center 54
- 3. Handwriting Center 56
- 4. Math Center 58
- 5. Listening Center 61
- 6. Geography Center 62
- 7. Communication Center 66
- 8. Art Center 70

Reproducibles
- Toy-Tote Instructions
  - Loop-Stick Toy Tote 74
  - Telephone Toy Tote 75
  - Picture-Puzzle Toy Tote 76
  - Funnel-and-Container Toy Tote 77
  - Underwater-Viewer Toy Tote 78
  - Kazoo Toy Tote 79
- Letters to Parents
  - 1. Environmental-Print Letter 80
  - 2. Story-Tag Bag Letter 81
  - 3. Toy-Tote Letter 82
- Patterns 84-97

Introduction

Are you a bag person? Bag people have special qualities. Here are some of them:

(1) A bag person must have imagination and creativity.
(2) A bag person must know how to use bags for things other than shopping for cantaloupe at the grocery store.
(3) A bag person must live on a "fixed" income and need to save money by using cheap stuff and recycled things from parents.
(4) A bag person must willingly assume the risk of being called "the bag lady."

It also helps if you are an early-childhood teacher.

One of the greatest limitations a teacher faces in running a successful classroom today is lack of money to buy essential materials and supplies. It becomes important to find ways to stretch dollars. Saving money is especially important to first and second year teachers who, being new to the profession, are exploring ways to save money while buying essential things only.

That brings us to bags. Bags are among the least expensive materials a teacher can use to make classroom activities. The ideas presented range from easy to difficult but are examples only. You can change them to use with any topic or to teach any skill. They can be geared to suit the different ability levels and skills of the diverse group of children in your classroom.

About state standards: they are here to stay or on the way. They are not that hard to deal with anyway. So, relax and read on.

Standards are the operational definitions of the skills your children need to master by a certain time or grade level. To simplify things, think of skills as standards in the process of being met through the activities your children do. Most of you have always looked for skills because skill development is what school is all about.

While state standards are worded differently from state to state, many core elements are similar. Some states have standards for most curriculum areas, while other states have standards for just a few, like for reading and math. Standards are similar enough from state to state, however, to assume that you can integrate them into your current practices in most settings

So what's in the book?

There are more than 65 activities in the Activities in Bags and Centers in Bags sections. The Reproducibles section contains more activities using Toy Totes and Letters-to-Parents discussing environmental print, Story-Tag Bags, and Toy Totes. There is a Patterns section, as well, at the back of the book that will make it easier for you to use these activities in your classroom now.

A list of state standards that apply to each activity is at the end of each activity. The list is useful because it makes you aware of all the skills the children learn by doing the activities. Knowledge of skills learned will help you prepare lesson plans that meet state standards. Pointing to the list will also help you justify to others why doing these apparently simple activities using bags is such a useful educational approach with young children.

Remember, you are a bag person. You have special qualities. Your most special quality is being an early childhood teacher. Enjoy using these bag ideas in your classroom.

Activities in Bags

1. Puppets

Hand puppets help fill children's days with conversations and characters—to act out stories—talking their way through plots with expression. This is the stuff of literacy because it invites varied means of expression by the children through not only words, but also non-verbal communication, like hand gestures and facial expressions. Talking through the hand puppet children more easily express themselves.

It is easy to make hand puppets with brown-paper lunch bags. Figure 1 is a hand puppet of a cow. You'll see how to make it in Figure 2. The pattern for the cow puppet is in the Patterns section in the back of this book. To make hand puppets of other animals, find magazine pictures and enlarge them. Cut out the animals and piece them together. If you are missing some of the parts of an animal, improvise by making the parts from paper, coloring and cutting them out and assembling the pieces to make the whole animal. Teach the children to sing songs that go along with the hand-puppet animal. For example, with the cow puppet, use *What the Animals Said!* shown on page 5. There are many other songs you can sing for the various animals for which hand puppets can be made.

State standards that are met by using activities like this one:

(1) Uses words, figures, puppets, or illustrations to create an effective presentation or retell a story.
(2) Recognizes non-verbal communication
(3) Speaks fluently and expressively
(4) Uses complete sentences

Figure 1

Directions for Making the Cow Puppet

1. Color and cut out the cow-head parts. Glue the horns to the cow head.

2. Turn the bag up side down and glue the cow head to the bag flap.

3. Open the flap and glue the mouth at the fold line under the flap.

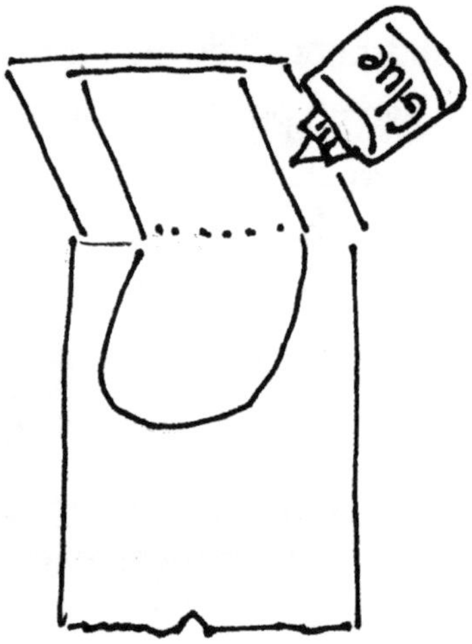

4. Glue on the tongue.

Figure 2

What the Animals Said!
By Sharon MacDonald
From: Jingle in my Pocket CD

"Boom, boom!" said the little black cow one day.
"Boom, boom!" said the little black cow.
Think of the shock when he tried to say, "moo"
When "boom" was the moo that he, could do.

"Glug, glug!" said the little pink pig one day.
"Glug, glug!" said the little pink pig.
Think of the shock when he tried to say, "oink"
When "glug" was the oink that he, could do.

"Toot, toot!" said the little yellow chick one day.
"Toot, toot!" said the little yellow chick.
Think of the shock when he tried to say, "peep"
When "toot" was the peep that he, could do.

"Plunk, plunk!" said the little white sheep one day.
"Plunk, plunk!" said the little white sheep.
Think of the shock when he tried to say, "baa"
When "plunk" was the baa that he, could do.

"Hey, Hey!" the farmer said to his brood one day.
"Hey, Hey!" the farmer said to his brood.
Think of the shock when his animals said
"Plunk, plunk, toot, toot, glug, glug, boom, boom!"

2. Storyboards

Storyboards provide the backdrop for stories set outdoors and indoors. Storyboards help bring stories to life and make the characters real. In time, the children learn to make their own storyboards as well as the story characters.

Initially, make storyboards yourself on large, brown-paper grocery bags. After the children understand how to make and to use them, ask them to make their own on large brown-paper grocery bags or lunch bags (please see Figure 3 for help making a storyboard). You can use the same outdoor scene from story to story, like with The Three Billy Goats Gruff, Three Little Pigs, and similar stories with outside settings. Make an indoor scene on another bag for use with all stories set indoors.

The story pieces are kept in the storyboard bag. When a child tells the story he takes out the pieces as he retells the story on the storyboard. When he is finished, he puts them back in the bag. Initially, you provide the storyboard characters, too. Photocopy, cut out, and laminate the characters. After the children have mastered making storyboards, ask them to make their own story characters.

Figure 3

State standards that are met by using activities like this one:
 (1) Retells a story from beginning to end
 (2) Retells a story independently, modeling patterns of changes in timing and voice expression.
 (3) Describes a setting, characters, plot, and solution
 (4) Uses effective language and style
 (5) Visualizes the information in a story and demonstrates this by drawing pictures or retelling it

(1) Start off using storyboards with stories the children are familiar with, like: Three Billy Goats Gruff, Goldilocks and the Three Bears, Little Red Riding Hood, The Three Little Pigs, The Gingerbread Man, Henny Penny, and The Little Red Hen.
(2) After the children understand how to use a storyboard, provide paper, pencils, markers, crayons, colored pencils, and scissors for the children to make the characters and props to fit the story settings.
(3) Encourage them to make their own storyboards for lesser-known stories.
(4) Use other materials like the ones listed below to make storyboards:

Aluminum-foil sheets	Cereal boxes
Pizza circles	Colored or manila folders
Old window shades	Old suitcase
Old Venetian Blinds	Old lunch box
Picture frames	Dishpan

(5) After the children have made their storyboards have them retell and dramatize the story to a friend.

Figure 4

A Fun Idea!

Read any of the books Popcorn Dragon by Jane Thayer, Popcorn by Frank Ash, or Popcorn by Tomie de Paola. Decorate one side of the bags with popcorn designs from the books and glue the cooking directions on the other. Have the children eat the popcorn and take the empty bags home to pop popcorn with their parent(s). Please see an illustration of the popcorn bag in Figure 4

3. Story-Tag Bag

A story tag is an object from a story or a symbol of an event in a story. It is a slice of the story experience for the child. They are useful to the extent that they remind the child of the story and bring forth feelings and thoughts about it that are useful in building reading skills.

Use large grocery bags to make story-tag bags (please see Figure 5). Story-tag bags support stories you have read in class or that the children have read. They can also support an event that the class has experienced like making applesauce or visiting the fire station. If you have read a story to the class, for example, put an object in the bag that depicts an event that took place or is a reminder of an actual event from the story. Here are some objects to put in story-tag bags for the stories you have chosen:

<u>The Very Hungry Caterpillar</u>: A plastic fishing worm in the bag (i.e., it looks like a caterpillar)
<u>The Wind</u>: A small, wood-and-paper umbrella (a novelty item, available at party-supply stores, often used to decorate exotic drinks).
<u>The Apple Thief</u>: A small, eraser colored and in the shape of an apple.
<u>Everybody Needs a Rock</u>: A small rock.
<u>Chester's Way:</u> A watermelon seed in a snack-size Baggie.

Figure 5

Take a fall walk around the school neighborhood. Find some interesting leaves, laminate them and put one in the bag. Save the rest to sort, graph, classify, and to make collages. The story-tag bag works like this: Each day a child chooses an item from the bag and retells a story, or an event, sequentially.

Add to your story-tag bag all year. When telling a story, have the child wear the story-telling vest. Wearing the vest makes him or her the storyteller of the moment to whom all the children are willing to listen for a short time. Here is how to make the vest from a large, brown-paper grocery bag (please see Figure 6).

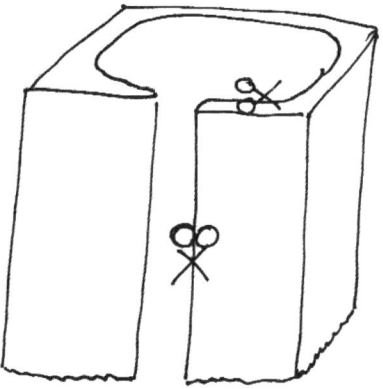 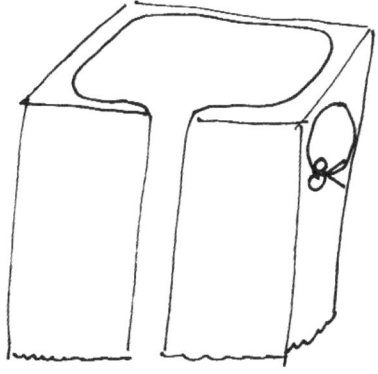

1. Turn the bag up-side-down. Cut a neck hole in the bottom of the bag. Cut down the front of the bag to make a vest.

2. Cut arm holes on both sides of the bag.

3. Draw a "Presenter" badge on the vest. Make a presenter-pocket with a *baggie*; glue it to the vest. Have index cards pre-cut to fit the *baggie* and pencils available. When a child is the Presenter, ask him to write his name on the card and slide it into the *baggie*.

Figure 6

A Parent Component to the Story-Tag Bag

To involve the parent(s) in story-tag bags, send home a brown-paper lunch bag with the child's name written across the bag front. Write "Story-Tag Bag" beneath the child's name. Enclose a letter explaining that from time to time you will be sending items home to be put in the story-tag bag at home (please see the Story-Bag Tag Letter in the Reproducibles section of the book). Encourage the parents to listen to their child's telling of the story when the child selects one of the items from the bag, or when he brings home a new object to tell about.

Send story-tag bag objects home when you can find small, inexpensive objects that are safe for the child to have. The small fishing worm that looks like a caterpillar used in the example above, The Very Hungry Caterpillar, is a good selection. For an event that has taken place, laminate one of each child's favorite leaves he or she has collected and send it home to be put in the bag. Inexpensive items are frequently available at the Dollar Store, in the Oriental Trading Company catalog, party-supply stores and at flea markets. It may not be possible for you to send items home more than every month or two, since suitable objects may not be that easy for you to find. Do it when you can find safe, small, reasonably priced, story symbols and objects.

State standards that are met by using activities like this one:
    (1) Understands story elements
    (2) Demonstrates basic comprehension of the content of text
    (3) Uses logical sequence to accurately retell stories
    (4) Recalls information from a story by sequencing pictures and events; recognizes predictable patterns in stories
    (5) Retells or re-enacts a story he or she has heard

4. Paper-Bag Masks

Masks help children become the characters in stories. When they wear a mask they are more enthusiastic and dramatic retelling the tale.

Figure 7 is an example of a bunny paper-bag mask. Other puppet bags might be a pig mask to use with the story, Olivia, for example, or a bear mask to use with The Three Bears. Make the rabbit mask to use with the poem on page 12, Here is a Bunny, and make a frog mask to use with the book A Frog in His Throat. With the classic stories, like the characters from Goldilocks or the "Little Girl" from the story, The Gunniwolf, make the character from a large, brown-paper grocery bag and have some props to go with the character. The children put on the bag and use the props to dramatize the story.

Laminate the masks by laying them flat and running them through a laminating machine. Trim the sides and the flap using a matte knife or box cutter. Use clear packing tape to cover and protect the masks, like the area under the bag flaps.

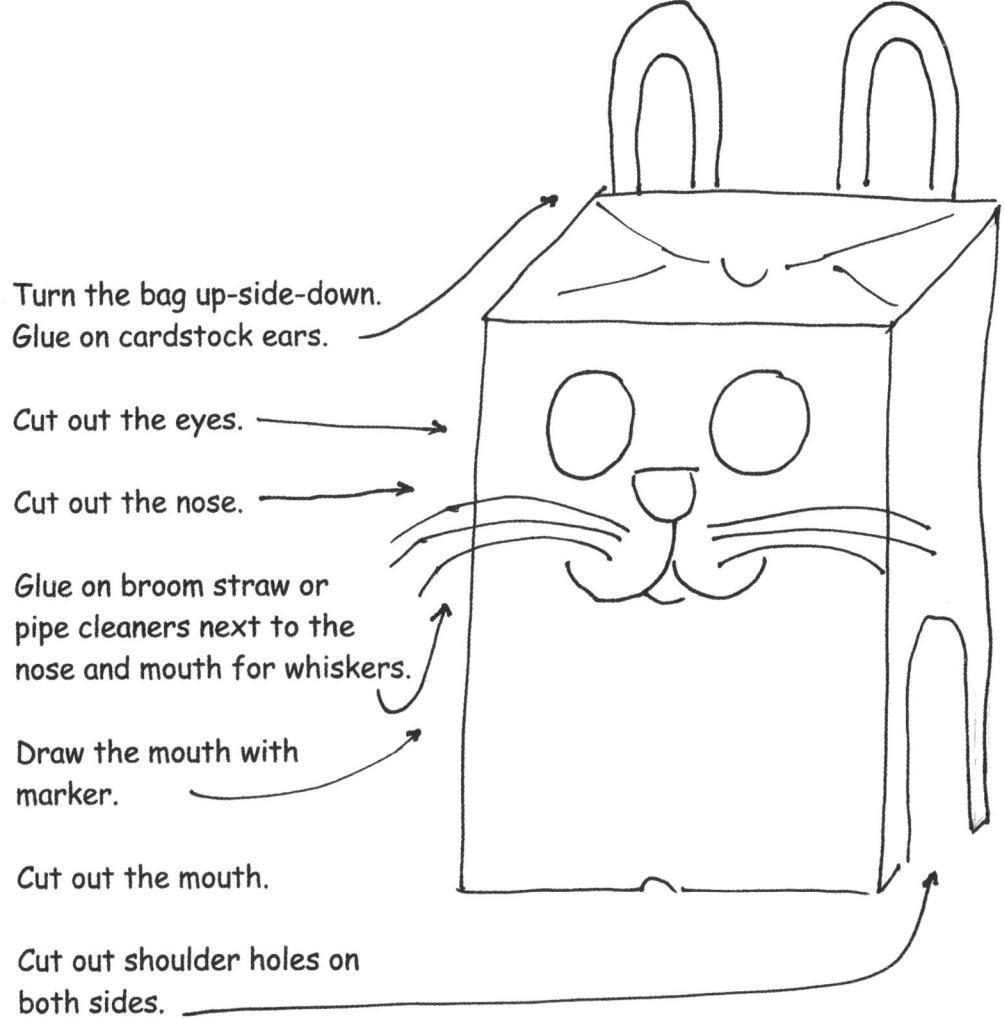

Turn the bag up-side-down. Glue on cardstock ears.

Cut out the eyes.

Cut out the nose.

Glue on broom straw or pipe cleaners next to the nose and mouth for whiskers.

Draw the mouth with marker.

Cut out the mouth.

Cut out shoulder holes on both sides.

NOTE: Cut the eyes near the top of the bag. Fit the bag over the child's face to measure for the location of the nose and mouth.

Figure 7

Note: Whenever you use story characters on the front of a bag, write the story on the back of the bag. The children will associate the story with the print.

State standards that are met by using activities like this one:
(1) Uses prior knowledge to express meaning
(2) Acts out the order of important events in stories
(3) Responds through talk, drama, and movement in a way that reflects an understanding and interpretation of the story.
(4) Displays knowledge of the beginning, middle, and end of stories.
(5) Uses appropriate voice tones, volume, and inflection for the audience

Here is a Bunny
By Sharon MacDonald

From the book: <u>Watermelon Pie and Other Slices!</u>

Here is a bunny with ears so funny
And here is a place that he found.
With his feet and his hands he digs in the sand
Makes a home in a hole in the ground.

Here is a bunny with ears so funny
And here is a carrot to eat.
With a munch and a crunch he nibbles his lunch
And slides down the hole on his feet.

Here is a bunny with ears so funny
And here is a log in his path.
With a bump, then a jump, he lands with a thump
And goes on his way with a laugh, ha ha!

Dance in a Bag!

<u>Try this too</u>:
Cut two eye holes in a large, brown-paper grocery bag. Have the child put it over his head and dance to the music in a bag (please see Figure 8).

Figure 8

5. Story-Telling Bag

Children need many opportunities to tell stories. Story-telling bags are a good way to get them excited about telling stories.

Figure 9

Cover the front of a small gift bag with soft-side Velcro. Glue the Velcro in place. Write a story on a piece of paper; glue it to the back of the bag. Make photocopies of the characters in the story; cut them out and laminate them. Glue a small piece of sandpaper, or hook-side Velcro, to the back of each story character. The children place the story characters on the Velcro as they retell the story. Store the story character pieces in the bag. See the Story-Telling Bag illustration, Figure 9, "This is the House that Jack Built." The children will associate the printed words with the story they are telling. When the children have lost interest in this story fold up the bag to use another day.

State standards that are met by using activities like this one:
(1) Understands story elements
(2) Demonstrates basic comprehension of the content of text
(3) Uses logical sequence to accurately retell stories
(4) Recalls information from a story by sequencing pictures and events; recognizes predictable patterns in stories
(5) Retells or re-enacts a story that has been heard

6. Lunch-Bag Diary

Children love secrets. The lunch-bag diary is a good way for them to write down their secrets. If you want to use the lunch-bag diary as a book, instead of a diary, use zoo animals as subjects. Put a drawing or a photograph of the animal on the bag flap, instead of the child's self-portrait. Have the children write about the animal. If you want to enhance a literacy program, put a word on the flap and have the children practice writing the word or write stories using the word. There are lots of ideas that lend themselves to the lunch-bag diary or book activity. Figure 10 on pages 14 & 15 shows you how to make the Lunch-bag Diary.

To make the lunch-bag diary, use a brown-paper lunch bag, two brads, crayons, scissors, a stapler, an 8-inch length of string and three sheets of white copier paper. Follow the directions in Figure 10.

(1) Lay the lunch bag horizontally with the open end (top of the bag) to the left and the bottom flap to the right facing up.

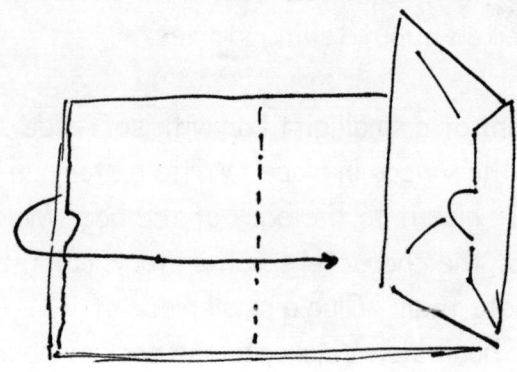

(2) Fold the top of the bag to the right, positioning the top of the bag edge under the flap.

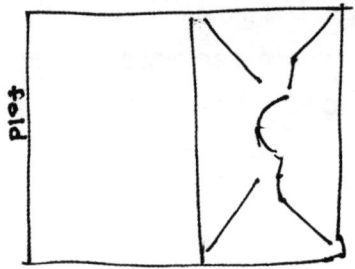

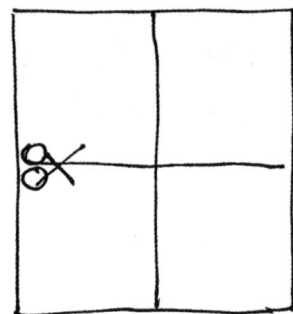

(A) Cut three white sheets of paper into fourths (i.e., you will have 12, quarter sheets of white paper).

(3) Unfold the open end of the bag.

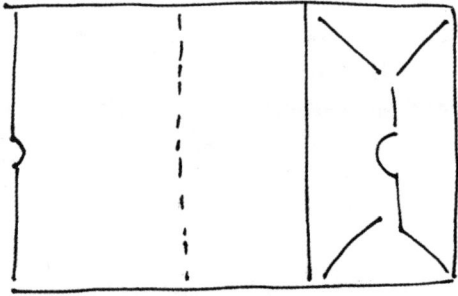

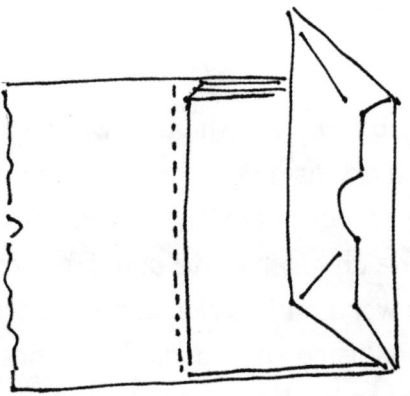

(B) Insert <u>eleven</u> of the quarter sheets of paper under the bag flap; position the left edge of the paper at the fold line.

Figure 10 (1 of 2)

(4) Fold the top edge of the bag to the right, over the quarter sheets of paper, positioning the top of the bag edge under the flap.

(5) Staple along folded, left edge of the bag (i.e., the quarter sheets of white paper will be stapled at the same time).

(C) On the remaining quarter sheet of paper have the child draw his face and cut it out with plastic, blunt-end scissors.

(6) Glue to the bag the child's own drawing of his face.

(7) With the diary closed, insert brads through the flaps (i.e., at the lower right corner of the left flap and the lower left corner of the right flap).

(8) Use a length of string to tie the diary closed.

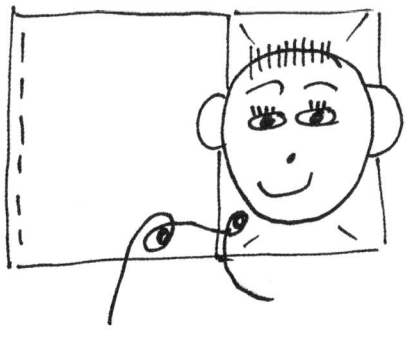

Figure 10 (2 of 2)

7. Stick Puppets On Stage

This activity is another way to excite young children about retelling stories. Cut off the bottom of a brown-paper lunch bag. Color the top half of the bag green, for the grass, and the bottom half brown, for the ground. Leave a one-half-inch border around the bottom of the bag (please see Figure 11). Make stick puppets for the story characters (please see Figure 13). The bag is the "stage" on which the stick puppet characters play out their story. The puppets are animated by the child telling the story, sliding the stick puppets upward with their hand through the top of the bag.

<u>Note</u>: You can represent the ocean by coloring the top half blue and cutting "waves" at the top with scissors (please see Figure 12). Color the top half of the bag blue, for example, to do the story <u>Swimmy</u>.

State standards that are met by using activities like this one:
    (1) Understands story elements
    (2) Uses puppets to help retell a story
    (3) Uses resources to enhance vocabulary
    (4) Recites short poem, song, or nursery rhyme
    (5) Uses words, figures, puppets, and illustrations to make an
        effective presentation

(1) Open the bag; turn it up side down. Cut a rectangle out of bottom leaving a one-inch border between the edge of the rectangle and the edge of the bag. Turn the bag right-side up.

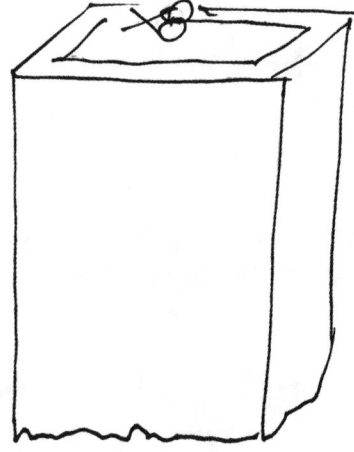

Figure 11 (1 of 2)

(2) Color the top half of the bag green (for the grass); color the bottom half brown (for the ground beneath the grass). Use scissors to cut a fringe (for the blades of grass) across the top.

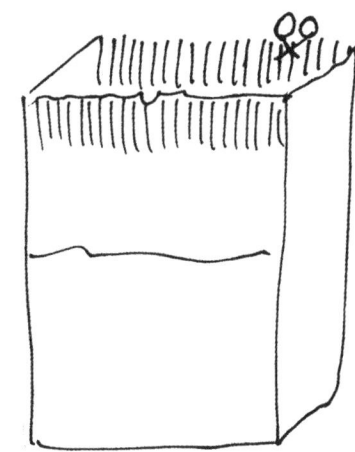

(3) The puppet-on-a-stick is pushed up from the bottom and it shows at the top.

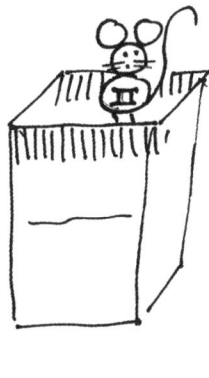

Figure 11 (2 of 2)

To make the stick puppets, photocopy the characters you want to use, cut them out and laminate them. Attach the jumbo craft sticks as shown below. To make other stick puppets, use the illustrations and examples (e.g., peanut, farm animals, fall words and rhyming words) in the Patterns section of this book

Figure 12

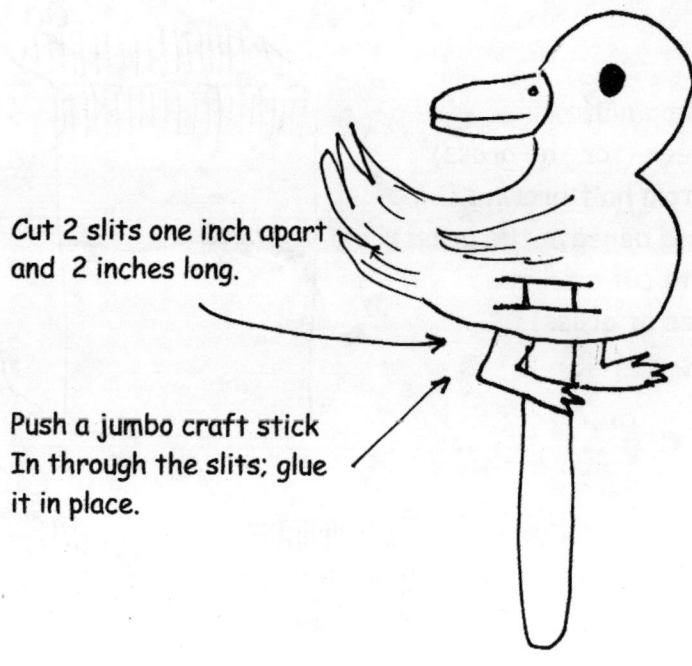

Figure 13

8. Tri-Level Book

Tri-level books help the children learn the topic words they use in class. Make them with small brown lunch bags (see Figure 14, pages 19 & 20, a tri-level book made for a study of peanuts).

Here is how the book is used. If a child cannot read the word, he can lift the flap and see a picture of what the word describes. If he is still uncertain about what the word means, he can reach inside the bag and find the actual object, or a close physical approximation of it. The migration from the abstract, to the pictorial, to the concrete is essential if the child is to make the necessary cognitive associations required to learn what a word means and then, to read. You can make a tri-level book for every major topic you study. The book gives children the opportunity to go back to the concrete, from the abstract, to reinforce learning.

The patterns for this activity are in the Patterns section of this book. You will find the words and pictures of farm animals, and for the fall season, in the Patterns section, as well. Find your own plastic or rubber insects and farm animals to provide the concrete experiences for your children. A leaf walk around the school to gather leaves can be helpful. You can pick up interesting rocks, too.

State standards that are met by using activities like this one:
   (1) Blends phonemes to say words
   (2) Understands new words from the use of pictures with the text
   (4) Reads to learn new information
   (5) Builds vocabulary through reading

1. Collect 4 small lunch bags, peanuts, pictures of each "peanuts" word you want to use, a hole punch glue, and a notebook ring.

2. Write the name "peanuts" on one bag, "seeds" on another, "peanut butter" on a third, and "sandwich" on the last bag.

3. Glue the matching picture underneath the flap of the bag.

Figure 14 (1 of 2)

4. Place the peanuts in the "peanuts" bag, two seeds in the "seeds" bag, a baggie with brown paper in it and Jiff written on the outside of the baggie for the "peanut butter" bag, and then put small sheets of white paper inside the "sandwich" bag. The children will draw a sandwich with the paper.

5. Punch a hole in the corner of each bag.

6. Put the notebook ring through the holes.

Figure 14 (2 of 2)

9. Rhyming Bags

Rhyming bags are a good way to motivate children to read. Use large, brown-paper grocery bags to make a book of rhyming words. Have a bag for each word, a hole punch, a notebook ring, and magazines to cut pictures from.

To illustrate how to make a rhyming bag, we will use the "at" word family and four large, brown-paper grocery bags (please see Figure 15). Use drawings, or photographs, of a cat, a bat, a rat, and a hat. Glue the drawings on the flap side of each bag, next to the flap. Write the word that matches the drawing under the flap. Hold up the drawing. As the children say the word, fold back the flap for them to see the word. You can reverse the placement, put the word on the cover and the photograph under the flap. Protect the bags by running them flat through a laminator, trim the sides and the flap and, with clean packing tape, tape the area under the flap. Drawings to use with the rhyming words for "at," "ig," and "og" word parts are in the Patterns section of this book.

FYI: The children can make their own Rhyming-Word Bags using brown-paper lunch bags and a notebook ring. Make one bag for the "at" family; have them draw a figure on the bag front that represents an "at" family word, like "cat," for example. They write the word "cat" under the flap. Inside the bag they can put other words that rhyme with "cat." They can add word family bags to their notebook ring throughout the year.

Figure 15

State standards that are met by using activities like this one:
    (1) Builds vocabulary through reading
    (2) Reads familiar text with ease
    (3) Identifies and isolates the final sound of a word
    (4) Identifies and isolates the initial sound of a word
    (5) Produces rhyming words and distinguishes rhyming words from non-rhyming words

10. Topic-Word Bag

Topic words encourage writing. Topic words are more important than others because they are the words used to build the children's interest and, like an umbrella, topic words unify the classroom in a logical way, not only for the children, but also for the teacher. These associations make writing easier because it is easier to move from one word to another. For example: "I went for a walk. Leaves came down from trees. It was cool. I put on my sweater." The words are related to the time of year.

On sentence strips, write the topic words you are working on with the children (e.g., pets, circus, and fall). With the topic fall, for instance, words come to mind like: leaves, sweater, apples, acorns, pumpkin, corn, and nuts. Glue a drawing, or a photograph, next to the object that the word describes. Place all the words in a lunch bag; put the bag in the Library Center (please see Figure 16).

If the child wants to write a story about something you have done, like taking a fall walk for instance, he can incorporate the words into his story. During the walk they may have seen leaves, nuts, and acorns. Ask the children to use the words in their stories and to look in the topic-word bag for the words they are not sure how to write. All of the topics you cover during the school year can be supported in this way. Drawings for all the fall words are located in the Patterns section of this book. Use the peanut and farm-animal drawings as topic words, as well.

Figure 16

State standards that are met by activities like this one:
    (1) Reads familiar words with ease
    (2) Decodes by using letter-sound matches
    (3) Demonstrates a growing stock of sight words
    (4) Understands new words through picture association
    (5) Classifies words into topics

11. Environmental-Print Reading Bags

To start children down the road toward reading, we need to ask them to read words they already know like the words from their environment. Children may not be fully conscious of the words they know already. It is easy to remind them. "Reading" such words makes them feel successful and to see themselves as readers.

Send a letter home to the parents explaining environmental print and how it can be used to help their child learn to read (please see the Environmental Print Letter in the Reproducibles section of this book). Useful examples of environmental print are: *Wal-Mart, Foot Locker, McDonald's, Big Gulp,* and *Walgreen*. Have the children bring their examples to school. Put each child's print in an individual gift bag and write his or her name on the bag front (please see Figure 17). Sometime during the day ask the child to read her environmental-print words to you. For a group activity, ask the children to read their print to friends and afterward, make collages.

Figure 17

State standards that are met by using activities like this one:
  (1) Recognizes common sight words
  (2) Understands new words from the use of pictures
  (3) Recognizes and understands words, signs, and symbols seen in everyday life
  (4) Uses pictures and associates them with words to aid comprehension
  (5) Reads information for a variety of real-life purposes

12. Creative-Writing Bag

We need to cultivate the creative potentials of the children we teach. We can do it through a creative-writing bag (please see Figure 18).

Put a pencil, a paper clip, a plastic star, a zipper, a clothespin, a key chain, an index card, a rock and a piece of paper in a creative-writing bag. Use objects that are similar when using this activity so the children can readily make connections between the objects they write about. Have younger children select two items from the bag, older children can select three items. Ask them to write a story linking the objects.

After a week or two of writing about the original items in the bag, send the bag home with one of the children to fill with objects to bring back to school. Ask the children to write about the new objects. After a week or two, send the bag home with another child to be refilled again. Continue the process until all of the children have taken home the creative-writing bag to fill.

Figure 18

State standards that are met by using activities like this one:
(1) Uses phonological knowledge to map sounds to letters to write messages
(2) Chooses own topic and organizes text
(3) Uses different sentence lengths and types of sentences
(4) Writes for self or for other audiences
(5) Uses correct subject-verb agreement

13. Baggie Books

Baggie books are a great way to display children's work. They can easily change what is displayed in the book whenever they want to. The children write stories and draw pictures throughout the year. They display the ones they are most proud of in the *Baggie* book. They can take them home at the end of the year, too. Having their work in sequence in a *Baggie* book shows the growth and change that have occurred during the year. You can make any size *Baggie* book and use them for photographs and even for autographs. Just select the *Baggie* size you need to contain what you want to display.

For smaller displays, like for photographs and autographs, use four resealable, <u>sandwich-size</u> *Baggies*, clear tape, a stapler, colored masking tape, a manila folder, white writing paper, and scissors. Follow the steps in Figure 19.

Baggie Book

You need: 4 resealable sandwich *Baggies*
  Clear tape   Stapler
  Colored tape   Manila folder
  White writing paper Scissors

With clear tape, tape the closed end of the *Baggie* to the table.

Lay the second *Baggie* over the first; tape it as you did the first one.

Repeat the process for the third and fourth *Baggies*.

Pull up the layered *Baggies* up from the table; fold back the layers of tape layers onto the back of the *Baggies*.

Cut insert pieces of manila folder to fit inside each *Baggie*; slide them inside the *Baggies*.

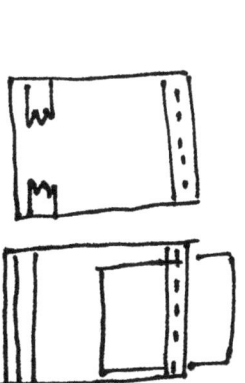

Figure 19 (1 of 2)

Staple along the taped edge of the "Baggie Book"; be sure to staple the manila folder inserts at the same time.

Cover the clear tape with colored tape forming the book spine.

Cut white sheets of paper to fit inside the *Baggies*.

The children write or draw on the white sheets of paper and slide them in the book. They can replace a page anytime. The Baggie Book works great as a photo album.

Figure 19 (2 of 2)

State standards that are met by using activities like this one:
(1) Chooses own topic for writing
(2) Rereads own writing
(3) Writes informally for various purposes
(4) Organizes and groups related ideas
(5) Combines pictures and words to tell a story

14. Lunch-Bag Tree

Follow the directions on the next page to make a brown-paper-lunch-bag tree. (Note: A special thanks to "Dr. Jean" Feldman for this idea!)

In the fall of the year, glue fall-colored leaves to the tree branches. In winter, cover the tree with liquid glue and sprinkle plastic snow on the branches (you can purchase bags of snow flakes, especially around Christmas time, at local craft stores). In spring, glue green leaves, apple blossoms, or red tissue-paper blossoms, on the branches (please see Figure 20).

Use a brown-paper grocery bag to make an alphabet tree. Attach alphabet letters to the bag like in the book, <u>Chica Chica Boom Boom</u>, by Bill Martin Jr. and John Archambault.

State standards that are met by activities like this one:
- (1) Recognizes the characteristics of a cycle
- (2) Recognizes letters
- (3) Creates artwork in all forms
- (4) Develops fine-motor skills
- (5) Aware of attributes of living things

Idea: Take a Walk!
Take a fall walk with small lunch bags and collects the signs of fall.

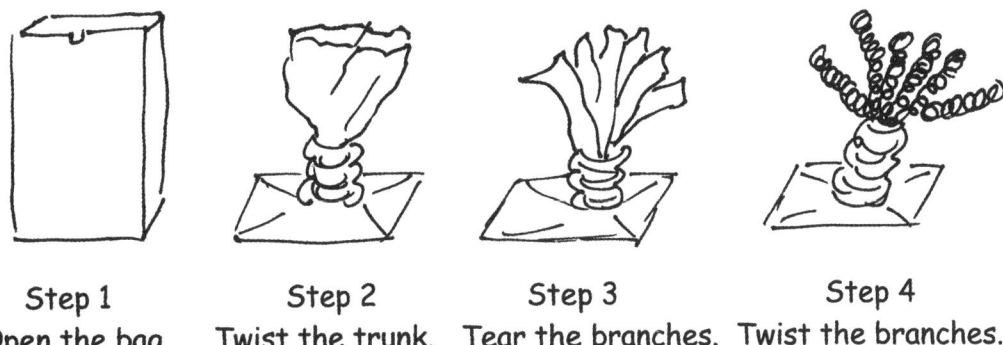

Step 1 Open the bag.
Step 2 Twist the trunk.
Step 3 Tear the branches.
Step 4 Twist the branches.

Figure 20

15. Sequence-Board Bag

Use a sequence-board bag to show step-by-step activities, stories, and life cycles in pictures. The butterfly life cycle in Figure 21 is a good example; it's drawn on a brown-paper lunch bag. Each box represents a unique stage in the cycle. This approach works well for subjects you cover during the year, like the pumpkin, frog, and caterpillar life cycles. Store the story-sequence drawings in the bag.

The brief story, told with sequence-board drawings or pictures, can be used to explain cooking applesauce, taking a fall walk, making a collage, or another task that can be explained in a brief pictorial series of steps. The drawings for making the butterfly, pumpkin, and frog life-cycle activities are in the Patterns section of this book.

State standards that are met by using activities like this one:
- (1) Uses properties depicted in pictures to sort attributes of natural objects
- (2) Explains the cycle of objects in nature
- (3) Identifies parts of a cycle
- (4) Knows that living things depend on the natural environment
- (5) Distinguishes living organisms from nonliving objects, and uses characteristics to sort common organisms into plant and animal groups

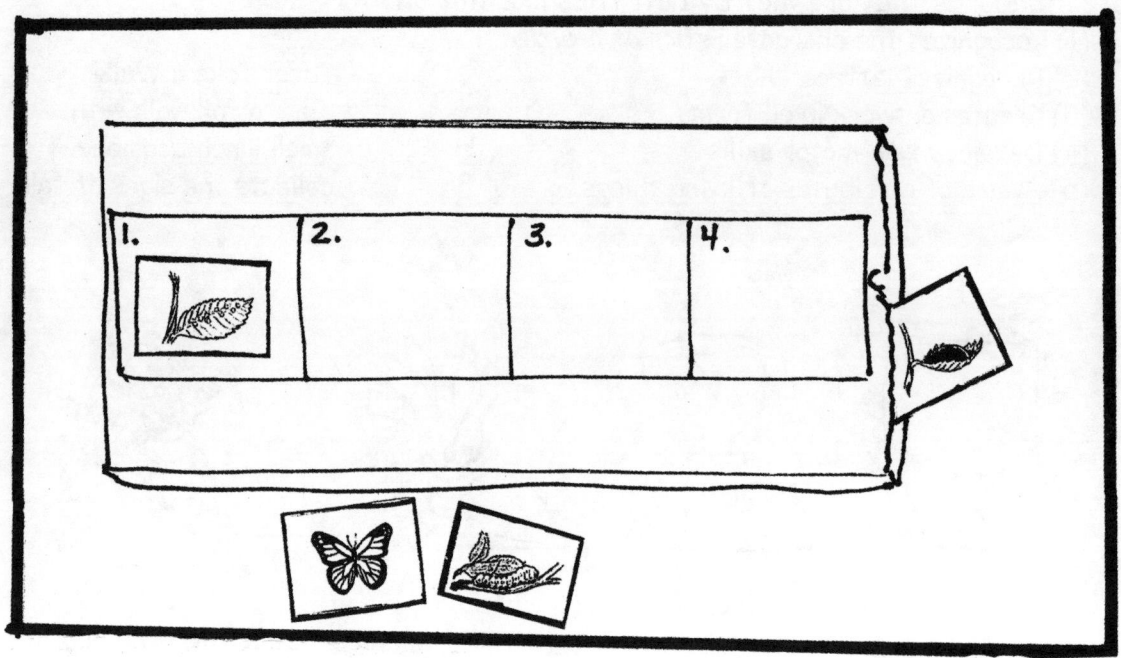

Figure 21

16. What's in the Bag?

Find a picture or a drawing of a pet, a machine, a flower garden, or some other topic you are studying. Make sure the picture can fit conveniently into a brown-paper lunch bag. You will need two copies; one will be glued in the bag; reduce the other to a one-inch square and glue it under the bag flap.

Glue the small copy under the bag flap. Reduce the picture on a copier, if necessary. It should be completely concealed. Glue the large copy to the inside back panel of the bag. Cut out several 1/2-inch holes in the front of the bag, over interesting parts of the picture beneath. Glue the bag closed. Ask the children to look through the holes and try to guess what the picture is about. At the end of the day have the children check their guesses by looking under the flap to see the picture (please see Figure 22).

Note: Laminate the bag by laying it flat and running it through a laminator. Trim the sides and cut open the flap. Use clear packing tape to cover the bag surface under the flap. For younger children, make the holes larger and have several more of them to see through. For older children, make one or two small holes.

Look

Guess

Check

Figure 22
State standards that are met by using activities like this one:
    (1) Makes predictions using prior knowledge
    (2) Examines the parts that make up the whole
    (3) Understands and uses guesses and searches for patterns
    (4) Applies appropriate methods to arrive at a solution
    (5) Interprets and compares information

17. Checkerboard Bag

Make a checkerboard bag to use for playing checkers. There are sixty-four squares on a board with colors alternating red and black. Use a large, brown-paper grocery bag and the lids from plastic water bottles or milk jugs. Use two different colored lids or spray paint the lids black and red--the red go on the black squares; the black on the red squares. The children play checkers on the checkerboard bag and store the checker pieces inside the bag.

State standards that are met by using activities like this one:
    (1) Understands the location of objects relative to other objects
    (2) Uses trial and error to solve problems
    (3) Checks for the reasonableness of results
    (4) Works cooperatively and collaboratively with others

18. Paper-Bag Kite

When you do a study of the wind, fly kites with the children. They will learn how the wind works in a hurry. It is hard, however, for each child to patiently wait his turn to hold the kite string of the principal kite you are flying, so make small kites for each child to fly until their turn to fly the big one comes around. Make the kites from brown-paper lunch bags, hole reinforcers, scissors, tape, a hole punch, and string. Follow the construction instructions in Figure 23, pages 31 & 32.

State standards that are met by using activities like this one:
    (1) Describes the relative motion of objects
    (2) Understands that energy comes in many forms
    (3) Understands causality
    (4) Understands how the parts of the human body work together
    (5) Understands that wind is moving air

1. Open the bag, turn it upside down; cut off the bottom.

2. Cut an "X" on the seam-side of the bag so that the midpoint of the "X" lies above the center of the bag.

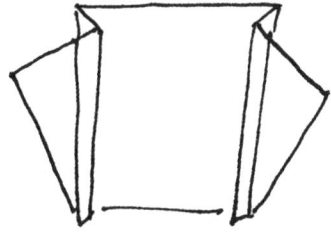

3. Rotate the bag 180 degrees. Open the wings; tape them to the front of the bag.

4. Cut a 2" triangular air vent in the back, near the bottom of the kite.

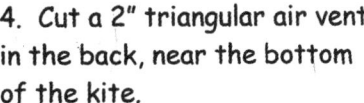

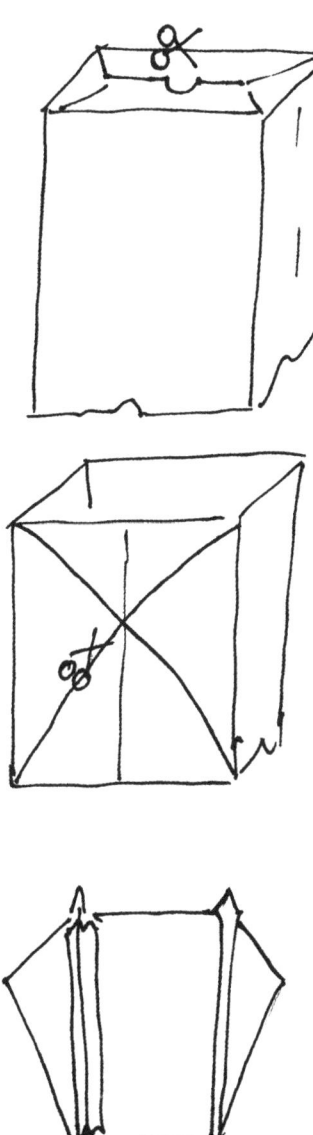

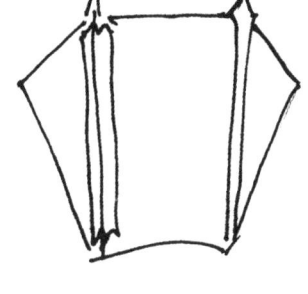

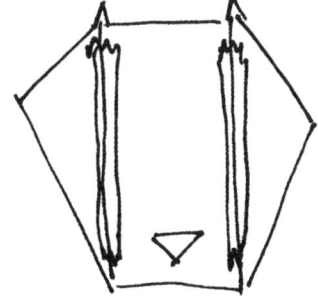

Figure 23 (1 of 2)

5. Make two holes, one at the apex of each of the bag wings. Put hole reinforcers over each hole on the front and back.

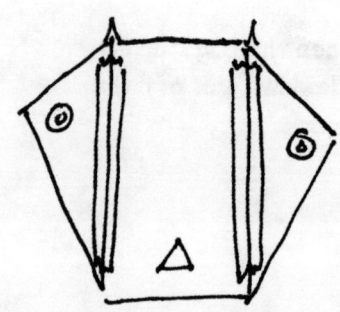

6. Tie the same length of string to each hole; tie the two strings to the kite string.

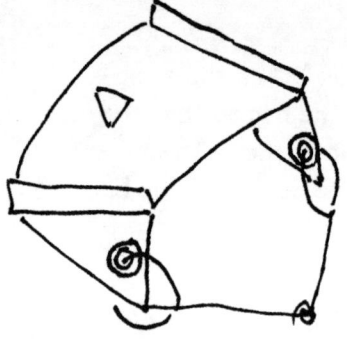

7. Fly the kite!

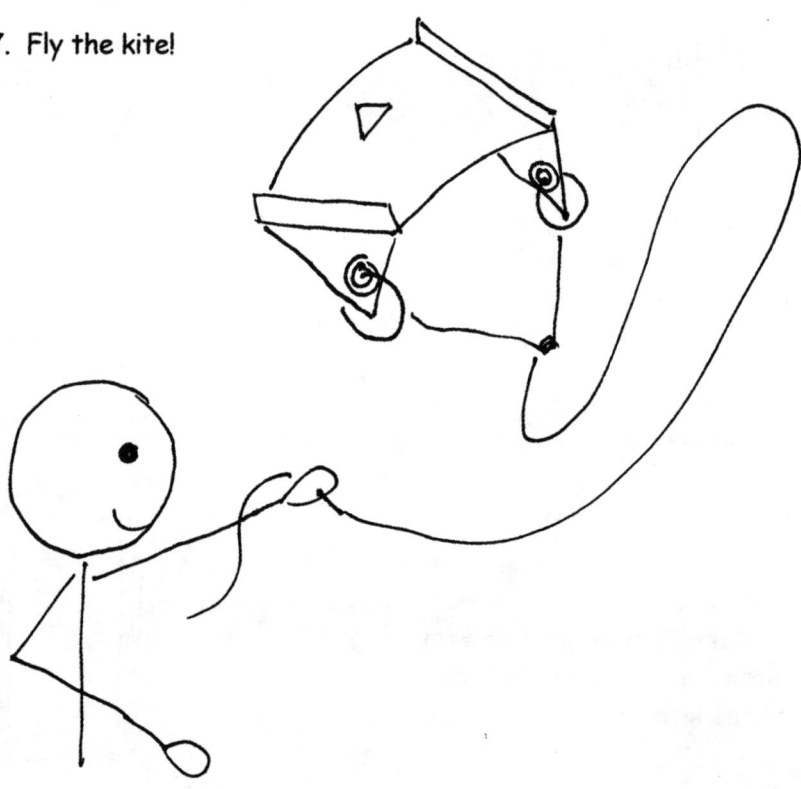

Figure 23 (2 of 2)

19. Paper-Bag Flower Pot

Children need many opportunities to observe life cycles--to see, and to learn about the natural world that supports life in its varied forms. Planting seeds is the beginning lesson of stewardship and of nurturing—important skills for children to learn. If one is to plant seeds in the classroom one must have a flowerpot.

Make a paper-bag flowerpot, Figure 24, by rolling down the sides of a brown-paper lunch bag to about 2-3 inches from the bottom. Fill the bag with soil and plant a seed. Mist it, <u>please don't pour-in the water</u>. When the seed sprouts, send it home with the child to plant, bag and plant together. The plant will keep in the bag for about two weeks. After that, the bottom disintegrates.

Figure 24

State standards that are met by using activities like this one:
    (1) Understands concepts of perimeter, area, and volume
    (2) Measures quantities using standard measuring tools
    (3) Makes inferences based on prior knowledge
    (4) Checks reasonableness of results
    (5) Distinguishes living organisms from nonliving things, and uses characteristics to sort living organisms into plant and animal groups

A Fun Idea: Make a Bird's Nest! Roll down all the sides of a brown-paper lunch bag until it looks like a bird's nest. Go outside to gather twigs, leaves, string, and cut grass to glue in the nest (bring some dryer vent lint from home to add to the nest!).

Figure 25

20. All-About-Me Box

It is important for children to learn to appreciate themselves, the most important person in their lives over the long term. Truly, one must learn to care about oneself if one is to care about others.

To do this activity, each child needs a brown-paper lunch bag; the child draws his face on the front of the bag. Using blunt-end scissors cut down the creases at the four corners of the bag. Fold the side panels into the bag; fold the top front panel into a box top and tuck it into the bag. You will have the upper rear panel of the bag remaining. Cut it into strips of "hair" and curl the hair on a pencil. Please see Figure 26, pages 35 & 36 for folding, cutting, and curling instructions. The child can use the paper-bag box to:

(1) Write facts about himself on strips of paper; drop them into the box
(2) Write descriptive words about herself; drop them in the box
(3) Draw small pictures of things she can do, put the pictures in the box
(4) Name the parts of his face and body; put them in the box
(5) Store special items from home. The older children can write about them; the younger children can tell stories about them.

State standards that are met by using activities like this one:
(1) Organizes and records information
(2) Uses properties to identify human characteristics
(3) Uses characteristics to describe the human body
(4) Includes relevant details in descriptions
(5) Writes for him- or herself

1. Face the bag with the bottom flap facing you.

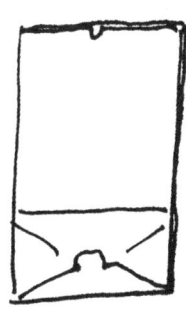

2. Fold the bag in half over the flap.

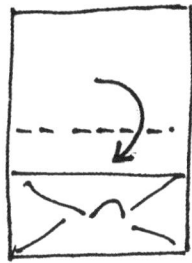

3. Turn the front of the bag facing you.

4. Have the children draw faces on the bottom half of the bag (no hair).

5. Unfold the bag; open it. Cut from the top of the bag to the fold crease at the four corner of the bag.

Figure 26 (1 o 2)

6. Tuck the two sides inside the bag.

7. Fold the front panel of the bag into a lid-and-flap. Fold it toward the back panel (the bag will look like a box with the back panel pointing skyward.) lid of the bag leaving the back section standing.

8. Cut the back panel into strips to make hair.

9. Curl the hair by rolling it on a pencil.

Figure 26 (2 of 2)

You can use the All-About-Me Box for other topics. For example, glue the picture of a frog to the top rear flap; cut around it and close the box. The frog will stand up at the rear of the box, "guarding" the information within. Have the children use boxes like this to store information about frogs (please see Figure 27).

Figure 27

21. Ice Cream in a Baggie

Children love ice cream. Figure 28 shows them how to make their own. Be sure to have extra time available—this activity takes a lot time.

Use resealable, snack-size *Baggies* and quart-size, freezer *Baggies*. Pour into the snack-size *Baggie:* 1/2 cup of milk, 1 tablespoon of sugar, and 1/4 teaspoon of vanilla. Put in the milk first, it will stabilize the *Baggie* and help keep the seal open to add the other ingredients. Add the sugar and vanilla. Carefully reseal the bag. Ask the child to mix the ingredients a little by shaking the bag gently. Slip the snack *Baggie* into the one-gallon *Baggie;* fill with ice and rock salt. Be sure the ice and rock salt surround the snack *Baggie*. Seal the bag tightly. Shake the *Baggies* for about 5 minutes. The ice will melt, so unzip the quart *Baggie* and pour off the water. Shake for another five minutes. The ice cream will not be as firm as store-bought ice cream. When it holds together like custard, it is time to eat. To make the time pass more quickly while you are shaking, sing all the songs you know and some that you don't know. You will need to keep the children occupied while they wait for the outcome. Are we there yet?

State standards that are met by using activities like this one:
    (1) Understands that printed material provides information
    (2) Uses pictures to make predictions about what comes next
    (3) Understands the scientific principle of irreversible change
    (4) Observes, describes, and records change
    (5) Uses sense of taste to gather information

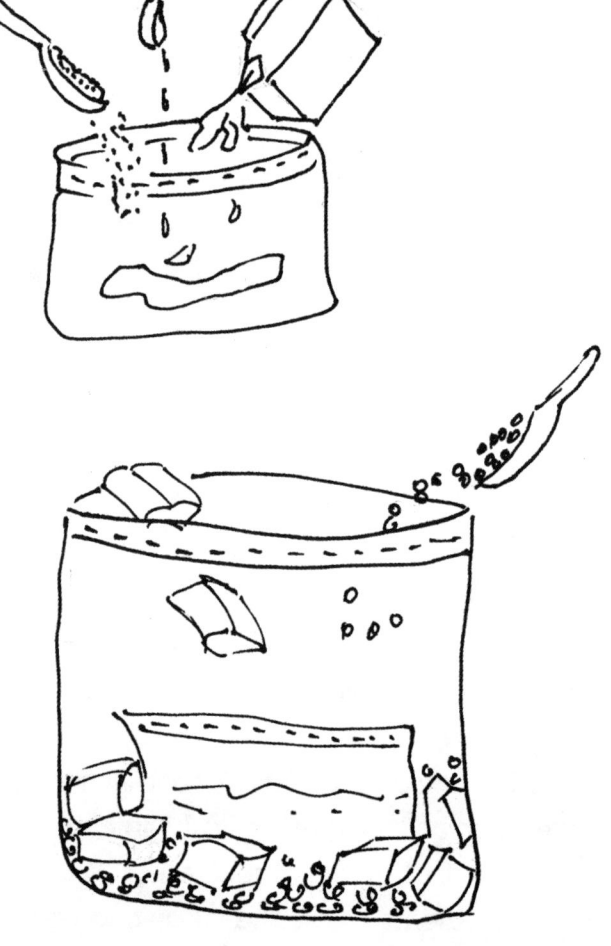

Pour the cream in small *baggie*. Put in the sugar and vanilla. Zip the *baggie*.

Put the small *baggie* in the large *baggie*. Put the ice and rock salt into the large *baggie* around the small *baggie*. Zip the baggie.

Figure 28 (1of2)

Shake! Shake! Shake!

Figure 28 (2of2)

22. Puzzle Bag

Life is a puzzle. Children need to learn to solve puzzles and to develop the flexibility of thinking required to solve them. Children also can learn that they can find many solutions on their own instead of looking to other others to solve problems for them.

Make a puzzle base with a lunch-size or a grocery-size brown-paper bag. Use a picture for the bag front that interests the children. Make a copy; laminate both the original and the copy. Cut the copy into as many puzzle pieces as your children can manage. Glue the original picture to the bag front (it becomes the puzzle base). On the back of the bag, trace the outline of all the puzzle pieces in the positions of the assembled puzzle; the children match the puzzle pieces to the silhouettes to help them solve it. Store the puzzle pieces in the bag.

With the puzzle configured in this way, you provide three levels of difficulty to meet the diverse needs of the children in your class. The puzzle can be solved by: (1) working the puzzle on top of the base (over the picture), (2) working the puzzle on top of the silhouettes (reverse side of the base), and (3) working the puzzle without the base. Please see Figure 29 for illustrations for the puzzle bag.

State standards that are met by using activities like this one:
(1) Examines the parts that make up the whole
(2) Understands the location of objects relative to each other
(3) Uses trial-and-error to solve a problem
(4) Organizes relevant information
(5) Checks for the reasonableness of results

Puzzle Bag
(Three levels of difficulty)

Figure 29

23. "What Am I?"

Make a "What Am I?" riddle-bag for various topics you teach during the year. On the front of the bag, write a list of clues describing what is in the bag. Put the actual item in the bag. After reading the clues, the child guesses what item is in the bag and then, checks her guess. Some examples are shown in Figure 30.

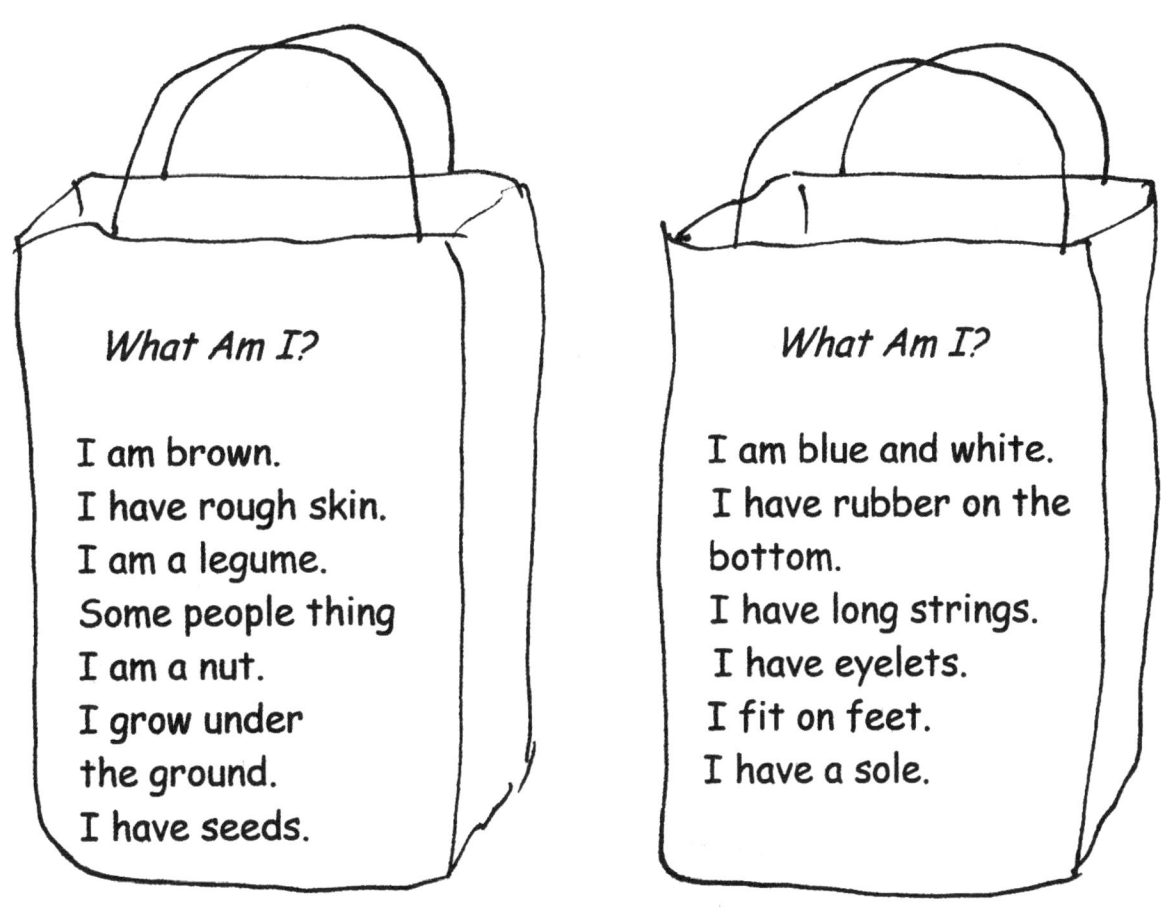

Figure 30

State standards that are met by using activities like this one:
    (1) Interprets context clues
    (2) Applies information gained from reading
    (3) Uses reading to draw conclusions
    (4) Establishes a purpose for reading
    (5) Makes predictions while reading

24. Questions and Answer (Q&A) Bag

Guessing is a challenge for children but it is essential to encourage them to make guesses and predictions, to check results, to make corrections, and to making new guesses and predictions. Doing things over and over, making modifications as needed to reduce error, is fundamental to how young children learn.

To make a "Q&A Bag," choose a question to write on the front of the bag and an answer to write (or glue) under the bag flap. The child guesses the answer and then checks to see if he guessed correctly. Two examples of questions might be: "Where can you find a bear in winter?" and "What are the colors in a rainbow?"

For young children, make Q&A Bags using a photograph or a drawing only. If you use the picture of a horse, for example, glue the front half of the horse under the bag flap. Let the rear of the horse show from under the flap. The child guesses what kind of an animal it is, then looks under the flap to confirm his guess. There are other examples of Q&A Bags in Figures 31 and 32. The first example asks, "What comes next?" (in a pattern). The second asks, "Who was the first President." If you use a question that does not have just <u>one</u> right answer, like: "What animal sleeps through the winter?" Put a picture of one of the animals (e.g., a bear) under the flap to provide one answer (there may be other answers). Have the children draw pictures of all the animals that hibernate to provide other answers when the Q&A Bag is used. Put the pictures in the bag.

State standards that are met by using activities like this one:
    (1) Interprets context clues
    (2) Applies information gained from reading
    (3) Uses reading to draw conclusions
    (4) Establishes a purpose for reading
    (5) Makes predictions while reading

Figure 31   Figure 32

25. Paper-Bag "Buildings"

For younger children, ask them to make houses, schools, churches, and stores, with brown-paper lunch bags and use them for accessories in the Block Center. For older children encourage them to draw buildings they see in their neighborhood. Use them as their buildings when the map their neighborhood. To make the buildings, suggest that they lay the bag with the flap side down to draw the windows, doors, and storefronts on the front of the bag (actually, they can draw on both sides of the bag, but they will need to ask a friend to hold up the flap to draw under it). After they finish, they open the bag and stand it up. The bag's open top is the "roof" of the building. Ask the children to make all the buildings--the houses, schools, churches and stores—in the same way. Laminate the bags by laying them flat and running them through a laminator. Trim the sides and the flap and use clear-plastic tape to cover the bag surface under the flap. If you use the bags as accessories in the Block Center put a block in the bottom of each bag to keep the bag standing up (please see Figure 33).

FYI: The paper-bag buildings can be used as a puppet stage by cutting out the bottom and extending the puppet figures out the top. For more about doing puppets with bags, see Activity 7, "Stick Puppets on Stage."

State standards that are met by using activities like this one:
(1) Understands that one object can represent another object
(2) Describes how people adapt to their environment to meet basic human needs and concerns such as shelter
(3) Understands and explains the roles people play in other people's lives
(4) Recognizes that people have jobs

Figure 33

26. Paper-Bag Streamer

Children love music. Music and rhythm give children opportunities to express themselves through movement: to act out what they imagine. They enjoy having something in their hands to express themselves as they dance and sing. Streamers are ideal for this purpose; they are easily made. Cut off the bottom of a brown-paper lunch bag and roll down the sides until the bag looks like a one-inch-wide ring. Staple crepe-paper streamers around the ring and leave a grasping space for a child's hand (please see Figure 34).

State standards that met by using activities like this one:
(1) Uses images, sounds, actions, and movements to express individual ideas
(2) Understands and applies artistic concepts to communicate ideas through rhythm, melody, harmony, tone, and dramatic action.
(3) Uses movement to keep the rhythm or beat
(4) Uses movement to integrate the opposite sides of the body

1. Turn the bag up-side-down. Cut off the bottom.

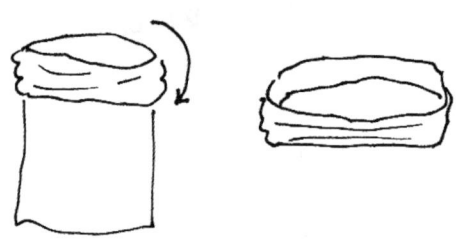

2. Roll down the bag until it is almost two inches high. (i. e., you will have a 2-inch high ring.)

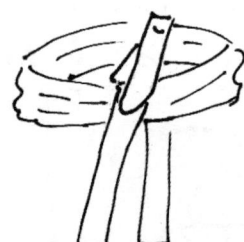

3. Staple the streamers around the bag edges.

4. The children use the Streamer for dancing, waving, and keeping time to music.

Figure 34

27. Art-Display Bags

About twice a year, teachers are asked to prepare for "Parents' Night." It is a time for displays and decorations. It is always a big hit to use the children's artwork. Using bags to display the children's work adds interest and it provides an easy way for the children to take home their artwork home when Parents' Night is over. It requires no pins, staples, Sticky Tac, or taping of displays to walls. Use grocery bags. Along the hallway and in the classroom, open grocery bags and stand them up. Cut large openings in each side of the grocery bag to display the child's artwork through the side. Put the artwork inside the bag; tape it behind one of the openings so the artwork shows through. Have enough bags for each child to have an art-display bag of their own or to display a small group of artwork done by the entire class (please see Figure 35).

Figure 35

28. Clean-Up Bags

There are more enjoyable activities than doing clean up near the end of the day. Few activities are more necessary, however. The children don't want much to do with clean up, so it is up to you to come up with interesting ways to keep them involved. Do it by using activities that tap into their interest in a multitude of things. Young children tend to be drawn to things they have not done before. A good approach is use a clean-up bag made with colorful, paper gift bag. Write "Clean-Up Bag" on the front (please see Figure 36). Place 2-3 objects from each classroom center in the bag. Have the children choose an object, put it beside the bag and go clean up the area from which the object came. When they complete that phase of clean up, they return to take another object from the bag. All the children continue until the entire room is clean.

Figure 36

29. Cares and Troubles in a Bag

Have a stack of brown-paper lunch bags available for the children to tell their cares and troubles to when you have more pressing things to do, like managing an incident that requires your immediate attention. After a child has vented into the bag, he wads it up and throws his cares and troubles away.

30. Toy Totes

Look for ways to get parents involved at home with their child's schooling. It is not an easy task, but Toy Totes can help get things started.

A Toy Tote is a grocery bag with toy parts inside for making simple toys (please see Figure 37). The assembly instructions are stapled to the outside of the bag. The directions are easy and the materials are common. Parents learn that useful toys, fun to play with, don't have to be bought--they can be made. In the Reproducibles section, you will find six Toy-Tote ideas. A letter to the parents explaining Toy Totes is in the Letters-to-Parents section of this book.

Figure 37

Centers in Bags

Managing Centers

Among the most difficult tasks of using centers in your classroom is coming up with a center-management system that works for you. A good system keeps conflict to a minimum and it is consistent and fair to the children. Resources are distributed through the centers to support a maximum number of children. A center with resources for five children, for example, will be chaotic if seven children are allowed to work there. Here is a way that has worked for me.

Use brown-paper lunch bags, jumbo craft sticks, packing tape, and hook- and soft-side Velcro. Each center has a lunch bag pocket posted near the entrance to the center. The bag has the maximum number of children that can use the center written on the bag. For example, if up to five children can use the center, "5" is written on the bag. When there are five craft sticks in the bag, the center is full. When a child enters a center, she puts a craft stick with her name on it in the brown paper lunch bag pocket and works in the center. When she leaves she removes her craft stick and moves to the next center.

To summarize, make one bag for each center and put the bag at the center entrance. Label the bags with one of the pictures in the Patterns section of this book. Write each child's name in your class on a craft stick. Store all the craft sticks in a can; put the can in place where the children can easily fetch their craft stick when center time begins. Please see Figure 38, pages 49-51 for instructions on how to make the bag.

Directions for Making Center Pockets

(1). Select and use the drawings for centers located in the Patterns section of this book. Make two copies of the center drawings you select. Color and cut out all the chosen drawings. To make one pocket, glue one of the drawings to the front of the bag, one inch from the top, draw a red line through the drawing (the red line "says": This center is closed). This will be your model for making the other pockets. Laminate the bag.

(2). On the front of the bag, cut downward from the top to the middle along the front creases, on both sides (the bag front is the side without the bottom flap).

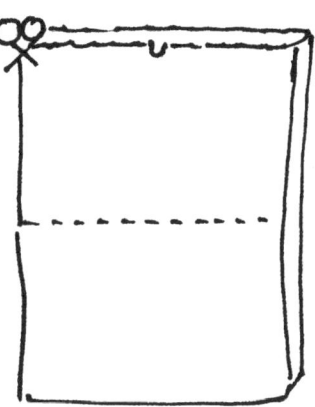

(3). Fold the upper front half of the bag over the lower half such that the top edge of the bag aligns with the bottom edge covering the drawing.

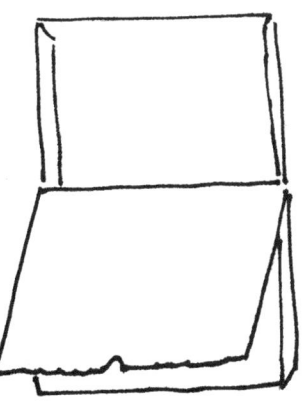

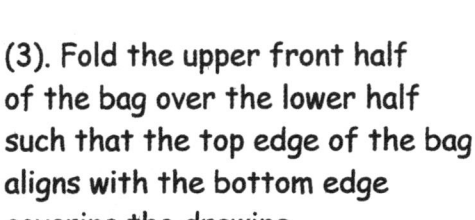

Figure 38 (1 of 3)

(4). Glue the second drawing to the inside of the upper half of the bag; write the number of children that can use the center at one time (e.g., "5").

(5). Tape over the second drawing, inside the bag, with clear packing tape.

(6). Use clear packing tape to tape over the upper half of the inside of the bag; tape down the side panels of the bag, as well.

(7). Affix a ½" square of soft-side and a ½" square of hook-side Velcro on the opposite inside surfaces of the bag about one inch from the top (i.e., the Velcro squares should meet to make a bag closure).

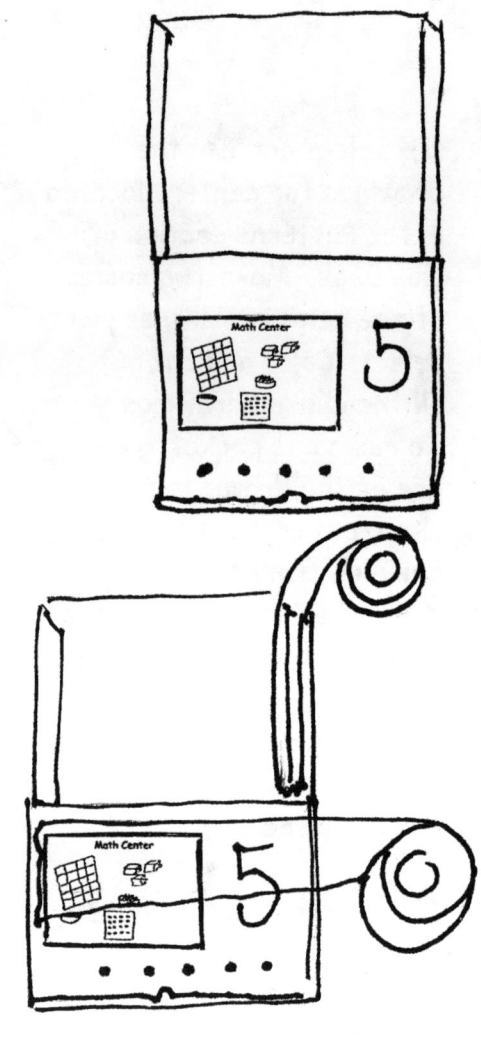

Figure 38 (2 of 3)

(8). Use a can of jumbo craft sticks with a child's name on each stick. When a child chooses a center, he takes the stick with his name from the can, chooses a center, and puts his stick in the bag. When there is the same number of sticks in the sack as there are children in the center, no other child can enter.

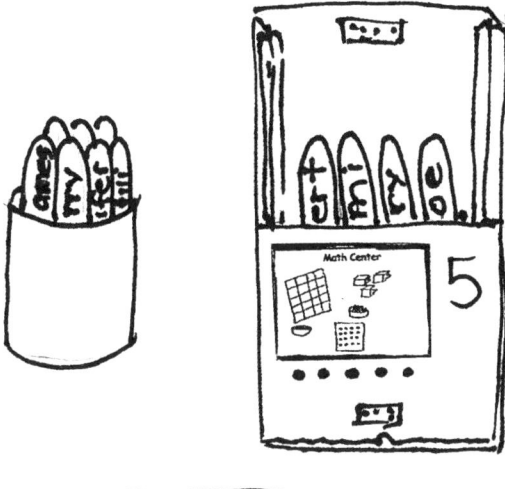

9. When you want to close the center, simple fold up the flap (stick Velcro to Velco) and the children will see that the center is closed.

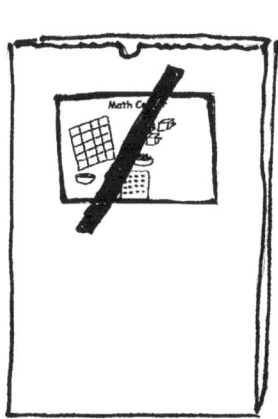

Figure 38 (3 of 3)

1. Working-with-Words Center

Building literacy skills is important. It is difficult, however, to engage young children directly in the process. We need to have fun activities that will draw the children into the action while teaching skills that make them reading-and-writing ready.

Label the front of a large gift bag: "Working-with-Words Center." Place the bag on the floor or a table under the Word Wall. The children <u>use the words on the wall</u> with any of the following activities in bags [please refer to Figure 39(1), (2), (3), and (4) for illustrations of these activities]:

(1) Magnetic letters in a resealable *Baggie* with a magnetic board. The children make words, sort letters, match upper- and lower case letters, and find all the "stick" and "hang-down" letters.
(2) Alphabet tiles in a resealable *Baggie* with a small, grid board. To make the grid board, draw the grid squares on cardboard, the same size as the alphabet tiles, like those on a checkerboard. The children use the tiles to sort and graph letters, make words, and play a game similar to *Scrabble*.
(3) A small container, about the size of a butter tub with colored, alphabet-letter noodles, tweezers, a jellybean scoop, and a small tray. The children scoop-up some letters dump them on the tray and make words using the letters they scooped up. Rule: They can only use the tweezers to move the letters (to improve pincher control).
(4) Alphabet stamps in a lunch or gift bag with paper and a stamp pad. The children do any of the activities described in (1), (2), and (3) above.

State standards that are met by using activities like this one:
    (1) Recognizes that print represents spoken language and conveys meaning
    (2) Knows the difference between individual letters
    (3) Knows the difference between capital and lower case letters
    (4) Understands that spoken words are represented in written language by a specific sequence of letters
    (5) Names and identifies each letter of the alphabet

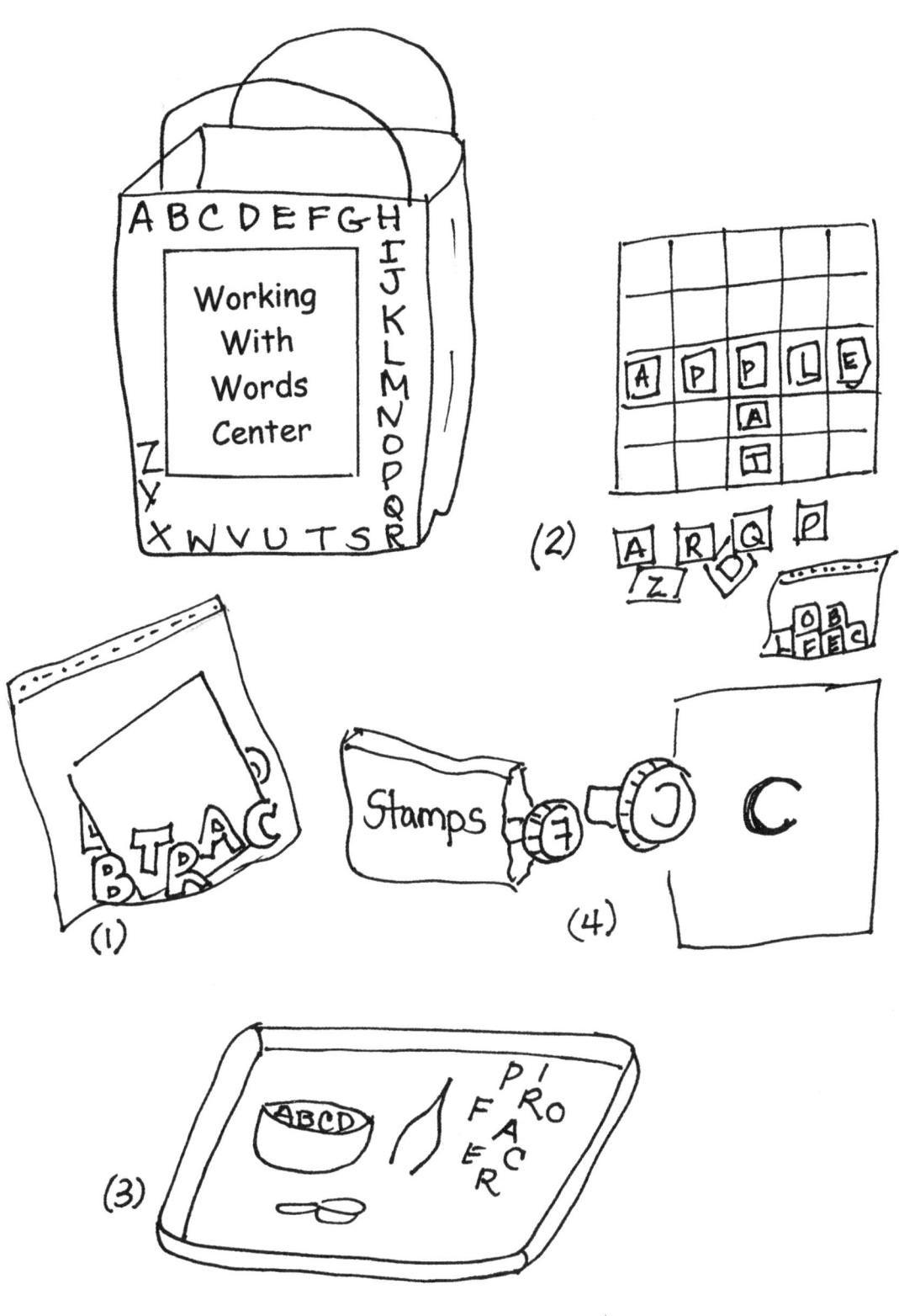

Figure 39

2. Spelling Center

Removing the skill and drill from spelling is hard to do. Making an interesting and inviting spelling center, however, is a good way to enthuse the children about learning to spell.

Write spelling words on sentence strips and put them in a large gift bag. Add these objects to the bag; as well, and please refer to Figure 40 for illustrations:

(1) A letter-of-the-alphabet, adding-machine tape. The children look at the beginning sounds of spelling words and place the words, one by one, beneath the alphabetized letters on the adding-machine tape. If they are able to do it, have the children alphabetize the beginning sounds without reference to the alphabet tape [see Figure 40(1)].
(2) Paper, one lead-, and one red pencil in a 2-gallon resealable *Baggie*. Tell the activity directions to the child, and write the activity directions on the bag. The child is to use as many of the spelling words as possible to tell a story. The red pencil is used by the child to write the spelling words that are used in the story. The remaining words in the story are written with the lead pencil [see Figure 40(2)].
(3) Write a few verbs and articles on short sentence-strips, put them in a lunch bag with the spelling words. Write the directions on the front of the bag asking the children to use the spelling words with the articles and verbs to build a sentence [Figure 40(3)].
(4) Put index cards, snack *Baggies*, and the spelling words, written on short sentence strips, in a 2-gallon resealable *Baggie*. Choose three spelling-word categories into which the words can be sorted. Write each word category on an index card and insert one index card into each of the *Baggies*.

Figure 40(4) shows a three-category example: (1) taking a bath, (2) school supplies, and (3) colors. The children put the spelling words into the correct bag. The word "soap," for instance, would be put in the "Taking a bath" *Baggie;* the word "yellow" would be put in the "Colors" *Baggie,* and so on. Write the instructions for this activity on a sheet of paper; tape it to the 2-gallon *Baggie*. If there are words available to use that do not fit into an existing bag category, have the child make his own category. Ask the child to think of a word category into which the words fit.

State standards that are met by using activities like this one:
    (1) Uses phonological knowledge to map sounds to letters to write messages
    (2) Writes messages that move left-to-right and top-to-bottom on the page
    (3) Uses words in more than one context
    (4) Spells age-level words correctly
    (5) Writes for a purpose

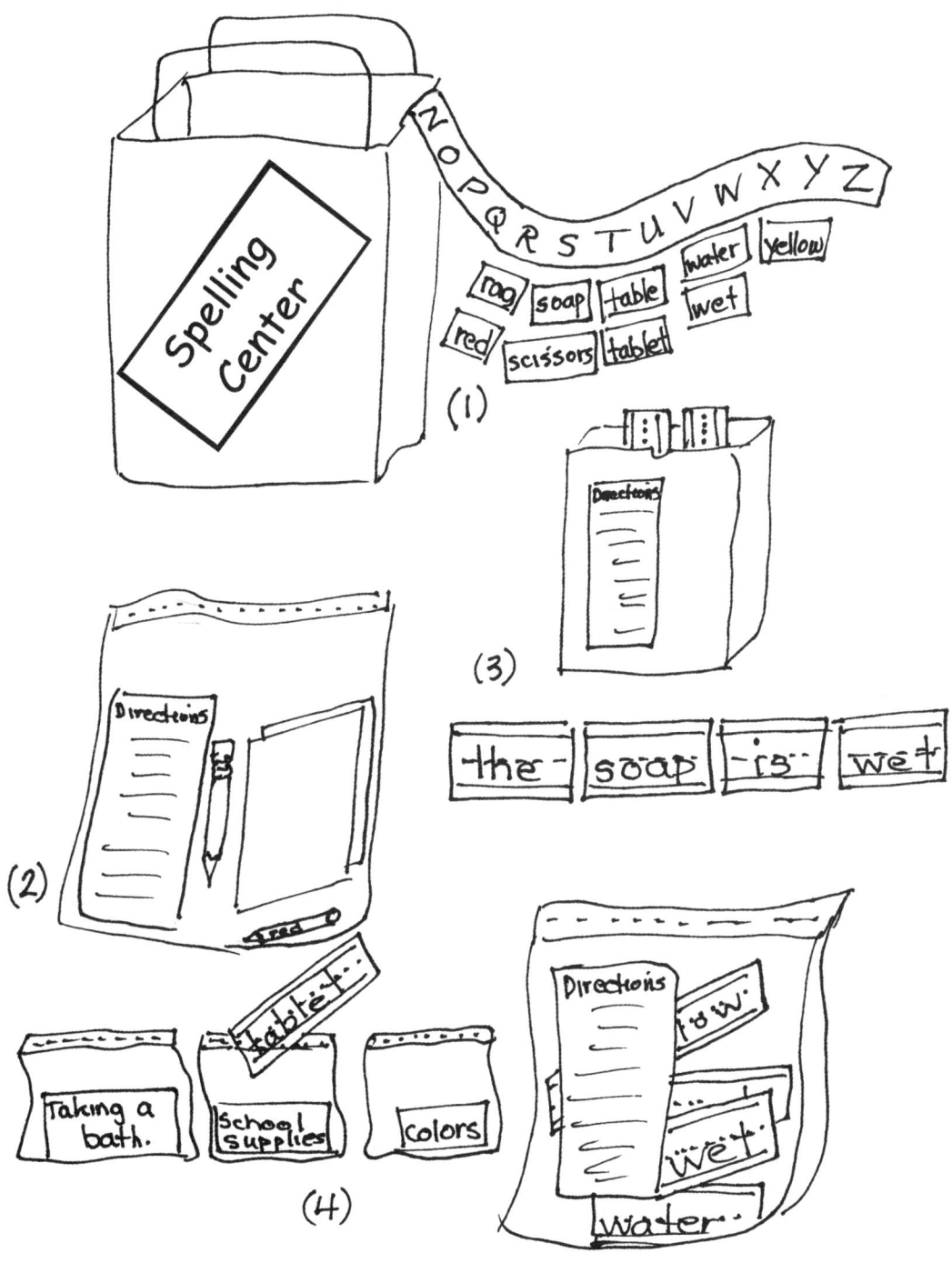

Figure 40

3. Handwriting Center

Using unusual things to make handwriting fun motivates the children to write. A bag filled with an unusual "thing" often encourages children to write.

Write "Handwriting Center" on the outside of a large gift bag. Put each of the following activities in 2-gallon resealable Baggies and put them in the large gift bag. These activities give the children opportunities to practice handwriting. Please refer to Figure 41(1), (2), (3), and (4).

(1) Mini chalkboard, chalk, and a sock (i.e., to be used as an eraser).
(2) Wipe-off board, dry-erase marker, and a sock.
(3) Gel pens and black paper
(4) A Magic Slate

State standards that are met by using activities like this one:
    (1) Rewrites own writing
    (2) Prints capital and lower case letters, correctly spacing the letters
    (3) Leaves spaces between words
    (4) Knows that print moves left-to-right, top-to-bottom
    (5) Gains increasing control of penmanship such as pencil grip, paper positions, and beginning strokes.

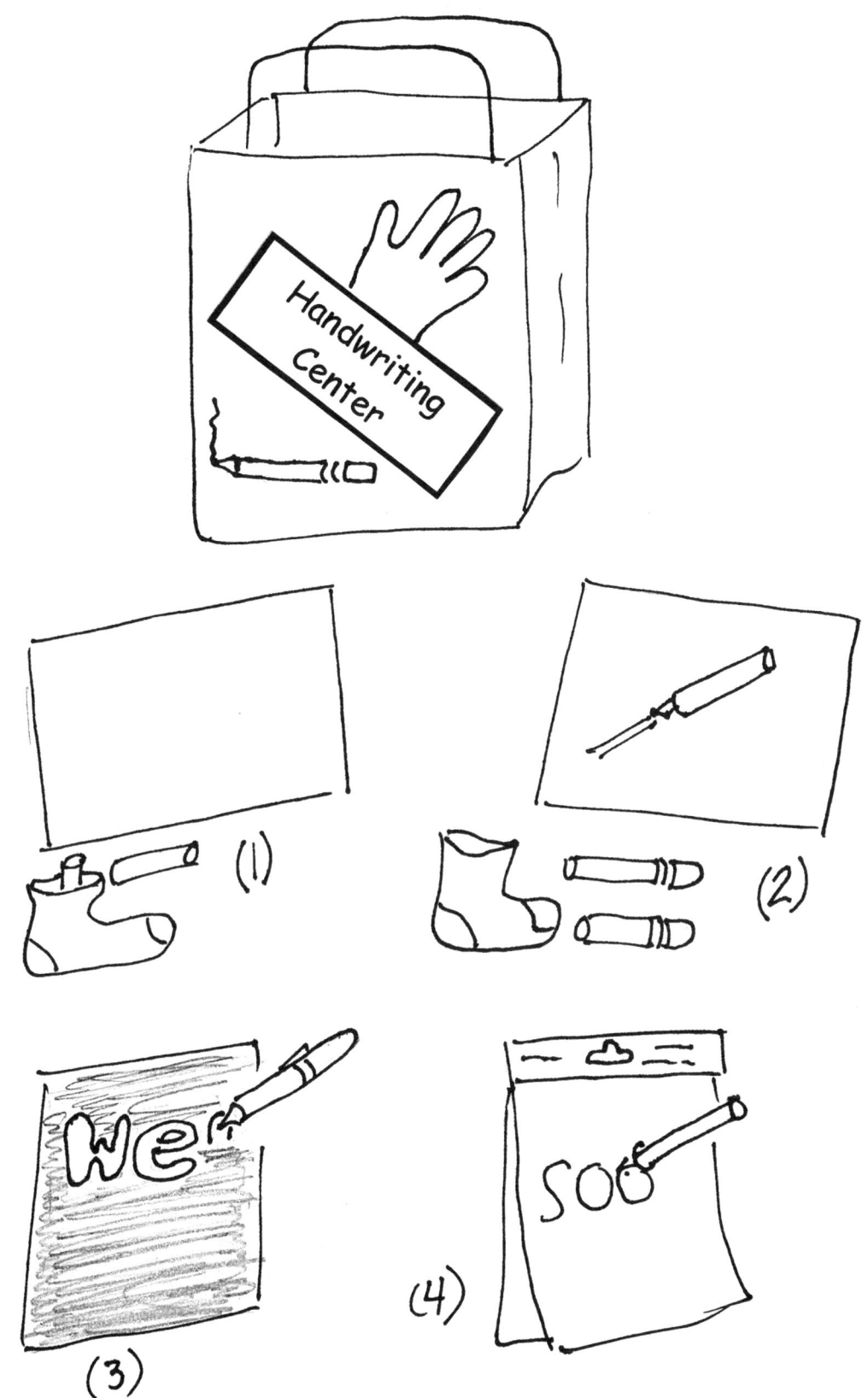

Figure 41

4. Math Center

A Math Center bag needs something for everyone—that way, a child can choose an activity that interests him.

Write "Math Center" on the front of a large gift bag. Place the following activities in the bag. Each math activity meets a different state standard(s).

<u>Graphing</u>
(1) On a small, gift bag draw a checkerboard grid. Collect an assortment of buttons, pebbles, coins, beads, and other small objects. Place them in a sandwich size, resealable *Baggie*. The children use the objects to graph on the checkerboard grid. Change the items to graph every week, or as often as the children demonstrate mastery of the graphing task with the items in the *Baggie*. Please see Figure 42(1).

State standards that are met by using activities like this one:
    (1) Compares objects by making direct comparisons with reference objects
    (2) Poses information questions, collects data, and records results using objects
    (3) Identifies, sorts, and classifies objects by attribute
    (4) Counts, represents and orders a number of objects
    (5) Makes tables to sort information

<u>Tallying</u>
(2) Put a penny in a sandwich-size, resealable baggie. Make lots of copies of the "Head-and-Tail Tally Sheet." Place them in a gallon resealable baggie along with the coin bag. Add to the gallon *Baggie* the directions to: (a) get a tally sheet, (b) get the penny, (c) flip the penny 12 times, and (d) tally the outcome of the coin flips. The outcome of the fifth flip is marked with a tally line across the four previous tallies. They compare their results with other children's results. For a copy the tally sheet and the tally instruction sheet look in the Patterns section of this book. Please see Figure 42(2).

State standards that are met by using activities like this one:
    (1) Counts and uses numerals
    (2) Identifies how objects are alike and different
    (3) Collects and organizes data into charts using tally marks
    (4) Understands that an object or mark represents a single item
    (5) Groups objects by 5s

Adding

(3) Color one side of five Lima beans with red paint or marker. Place the red-sided beans in a resealable, plastic sandwich *Baggie*. Make adding strips, like those shown in Figure 42(3). They are 3" x 6" construction-paper strips. Put 10-15 strips in a bag at one time. Put the sandwich bag with the Lima beans, a pencil, a small tray, and the paper strips in a one-gallon, resealable bag, add the directions. To do the activity, the child pours from the *Baggie* onto the tray the five Lima beans and then, counts the number of red beans showing. He writes the number in front of the plus sign (+) on the paper strip. The child then looks at the number of white beans showing and writes the number of white beans after the plus sign. The child puts all of the beans together and counts them. He writes the total number of Lima beans after the equal (=) sign. The child puts the Lima beans back in the bag and repeats the activity. Additional directions for this activity are in the Patterns section of this book.

State standards that are met by using activities like this one:
    (1) Demonstrates that "equal" means "the same as" using visual representations
    (2) Counts "how many" in sets
    (3) Explains addition using physical materials
    (4) Represents addition as combining sets
    (5) Writes number sentences to represent addition

Venn diagram

(4) Collect different types of shoes for work and play. Draw a Venn diagram on a gift bag. Write, "Work" in the left-hand area of the Venn diagram, write, "Work and Play" in the center area (where the circles overlap); write, "Play" in the right hand area.

The children put the shoes where they think they should go in the Venn diagram and they explain the reasons for their placements. For children who can write, have them make a name list of the shoes they have placed in each area of the Venn diagram. The instruction sheet for the Venn diagram activity is in the Patterns section. Also, please see Figure 42(4) for an illustration.

State standards that are met by using activities like these:
    (1) Organizes and clarifies mathematical information in at least one way
    (2) Expresses ideas using mathematical language and notation, such as diagrams
    (3) Searches for patterns in simple situations
    (4) Recognizes and explains how objects can be classified in more than one way
    (5) Compares and orders objects

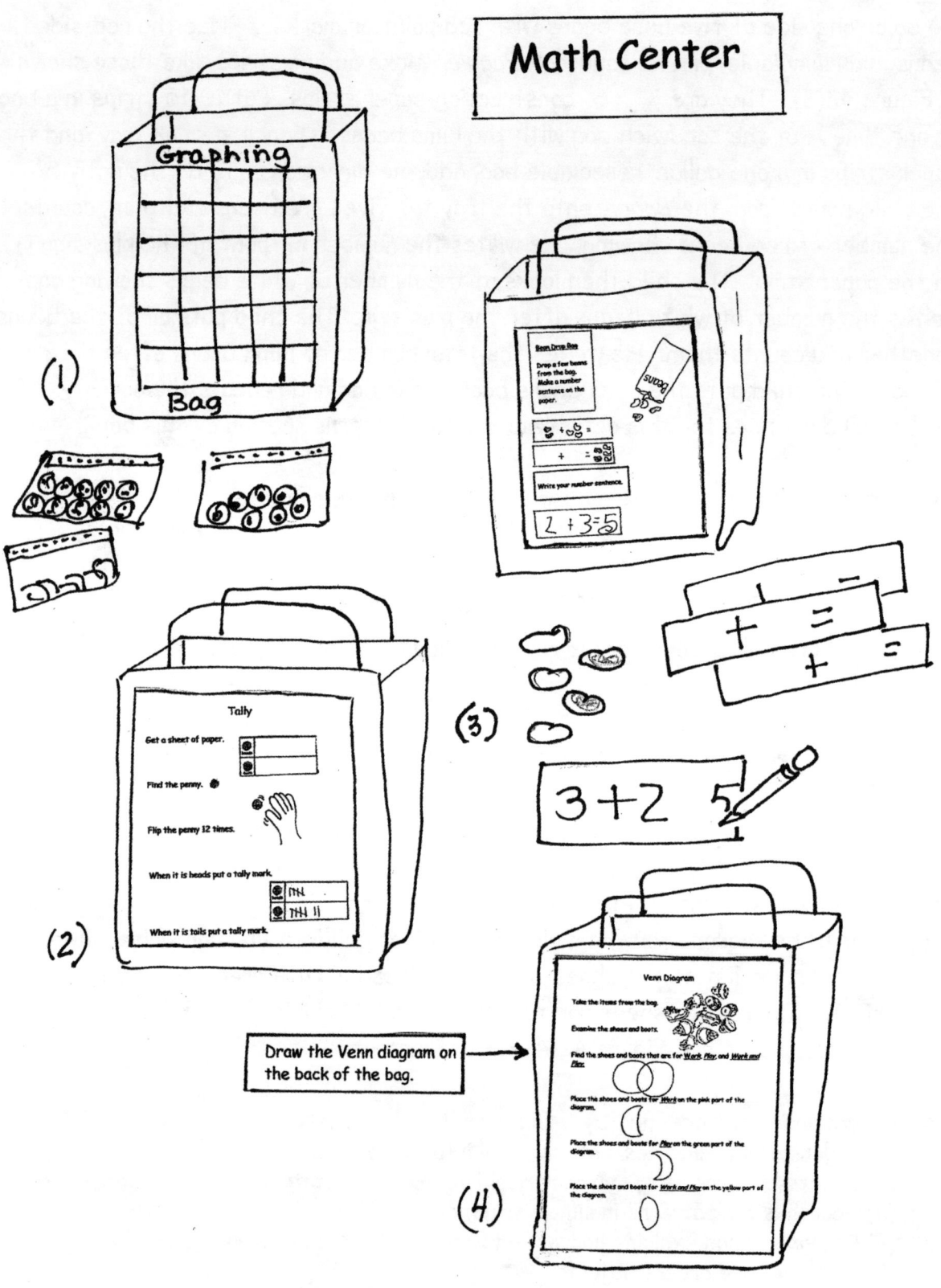

Figure 42

5. Listening Center

Organization is the key to keeping the Listening Center functioning well, so try this: Store cassette tapes with books in a resealable *Baggie*. Make a photocopy of the cassette cover and tape it inside the *Baggie*. Organized in this way, the children will easily be able to see which tape and book goes in the *Baggie*.

Keep a *Baggie* of blank, 5-minute cassette tapes next to the tape recorder; the children can tape their own stories or just talk and listen. Ask the children to erase their recordings after they have finished so the tape will be ready for the next child. Please see Figure 43.

State standards that are met by using activities like these:
    (1) Focuses attention
    (2) Listens and observes to gain and interpret information
    (3) Pays attention to oral stories
    (4) Uses effective delivery
    (5) Uses effective language and style

Figure 43

6. Geography Center

Geography can be fun for children. Take a look.

Label a large gift bag, or a brown-paper grocery bag, "Geography Center." Glue a small map of the world to the front of the bag (please refer to Figure 44 for illustrations of the activities below).

(1) Put in a resealable plastic bag: Continent stamps, paper, and stamp pads. The children stamp the continents on the paper [Figure 44(1)].
(2) Put in the bag several books about continents and mapping. The children can refer to the books [Figure 44(2)].
(3) Photocopy, cut out, laminate, and cut into puzzle pieces the continents from a World map. Color-code the back of each continent so the puzzle pieces are easy to recognize and put away. For example, put red sticky dots on all of the backs of all the Australia pieces and a red sticky dot on the *Baggie* in which the puzzle pieces are stored. Choose a different color for each continent. Store each puzzle separately in *Baggies*. Please refer to Figure 44(3). (Note: As an alternative, use the "Continent Puzzle Match" in the Patterns section of this book.)
(4) Have the children read the poems, *Globe* and *Where is Africa?* written below. Ask them to see how many places their fingers can find on the map on the front of the bag. If you have a globe, ask them to find the continents in *Where is Africa?* Please see Figure 44(4).

Globe
By Sharon MacDonald

A map of the world,
Laid out flat
Would not be a globe,
As a matter of fact.

But it could be, though.
If rolled in a ball.
They would call it a globe
With no corners at all.

Covered with lands,
Rivers and trees
And mountains and oceans
Whipped by a breeze.

In some places it's rainy,
And in others it's dry.
It's hard to imagine,
But you can, if you try.

You can see shapes.
There are color and line.
Can you name some places
Your fingers can find?

From: Idea Bags by Sharon MacDonald, published by Fearon Teacher's Aids, A Division of McGraw-Hill Children's Publishing.

Where is Africa?
By Sharon MacDonald

Where is Africa?
Can you tell?
It's there below Europe
Which is just as well.

Because below Asia
Would be a mistake.
There is not enough room,
For goodness sake!

Where is Australia?
I want to know.
Is the "Land Down-Under"
Above or below?
What do you think?
It's out there alone!
Knock, knock, knock!
Is anybody home?

North America, South America
And what's in between?
Hopefully not Antarctica--
It's not even green
It's made of ice
And it'll freeze you nose
And if you stay too long
It'll freeze toes.

From: <u>Jingle in My Pocket</u> Book by Sharon MacDonald, published by Grasshopper Press.

(5) Find a World map and laminate it. Place a piece of tracing paper over the map and trace each continent. Using the tracings, transfer the continent shapes to colored paper; cut and laminate them (use one color for each continent). The children do the activity by pulling out the World map and matching the colored continent shapes to the continents on the World map. See if the children can name the continents as they match them. Please see Figure 44(5).

State standards that are met by using activities like this one:
(1) Uses maps, charts, and other resources as a tool to gather information
(2) Locates places and major physical features of the Earth using maps, globes, and other sources
(3) Describes the natural characteristics of places and continents
(4) Recognizes spatial patterns on the Earth's surfaces
(5) Finds North America on a map and a globe

Figure 44

7. Communication Center

To learn to communicate effectively, children must exchange ideas and thoughts with other children. That is how they learn that much of what they think and feel is felt and thought by others, too. They also learn that talking about things helps them form new thoughts about the ideas they talk about. Make a Communication Center like the one described below and you will see the notes, messages, and letters fly from child to child.

Write "Communication Center" on a large gift bag. Put all the bags for making a mailbox inside plus, the bags for making envelopes, and the writing-a-letter bag (with paper, pencils, and the address book). The children make their own mailbox, choose their own P. O. Box number and send each other letters. Please refer to Figure 45 for illustrations of these activities.

(1) <u>Make a "Write a Letter" Bag [see Figure 45(1)]</u>
Work with the children to establish the pattern of writing a letter and addressing an envelope. Glue the instruction sheet to the bag front (please see the Patterns section for a drawing of the instructions). Put paper and pencil in the bag for the children to write the letters and envelopes [please see (3) below].

(2) <u>Make a Mail-box Bag [see Figure 45(2) and 46]</u>
Use a white, bakery bag instead of a lunch bag. It is easier for the children to use as a mailbox. Let the children decorate their mailboxes in red, white, and blue and come up with their own mailbox designs. Before the children decorate the bags, round off the top of each bag with scissors. Either you or the child, using blunt-end scissors, can cut a mail flap in the side of the bag as shown in Figure 45(2). Paper clip the top of the bag closed. Have the children write their name and mailbox number on the bag. Place the mailboxes on a shelf in the classroom. The children write letters, cards, and notes to their friends and deliver them to the mailboxes; they check their mail by removing the paperclip closures and looking inside the bag for all the newsy stuff that has arrived for them.

(3) <u>Make an Envelope out of a Lunch Bag [see Figure 45(3)]</u>
In a gift bag near the mailbox shelf, put brown-paper lunch bags, pencils, pens, markers, crayons, glue sticks, glue, and paper. The brown-paper lunch bags are used for envelopes to hold letters, drawings, and messages written by one child to

another. In the upper left-hand corner on the bag front, the children write their return address (i.e., the P.O. Box number they have chosen and their school name). They address their paper-bag envelope by writing in the middle of the bag: (1) the name of the child to whom he is writing, (2) the receiving child's P.O. Box number, and (3) the school's name. Have paper, crayons, markers, glue, and glue sticks available for the children to design and affix a postage stamp to their envelope. The paper can be used for writing notes, messages, and letters. The children tape or glue their envelope closed when they have completed their letters and notes and are ready to mail them. As a reminder of envelope style for the children, have the form of an envelope address glued to the front of the "Write A Letter" bag in Figure 45(1). You can find an example of the envelope style in the Patterns section of this book.

(4) <u>Make an Address Book</u>
The address book is put together in the same way as the "Lunch-Bag Diary" (see Activity 6, "Activities in Bags"). The variation is that instead of making a diary, make an address book for letters "A" through "Z"; one letter a page. Have a child draw a house on a piece of white paper; glue it to the bag flap. On page one, near the upper left-hand corner, write the letter "A"; on page 2 write the letter "B." Continue for all the alphabet letters. Ask each child to write his name in the address book, last name first, under the correct letter of the alphabet; also, to write his P. O. Box number and the name of the school. This will give the children a resource to go to the write letters to their classmates and friends without asking them each time for the address information.

State standards that are met by using activities (1), (2), and (3) above:
    (1) Reads own first and last name
    (2) Writes friendly letters or invitations that follow a simple format
    (3) Prints legibly, and spaces letters, words, and sentences appropriately
    (4) Uses correct capitalization
    (5) Follows simple directions

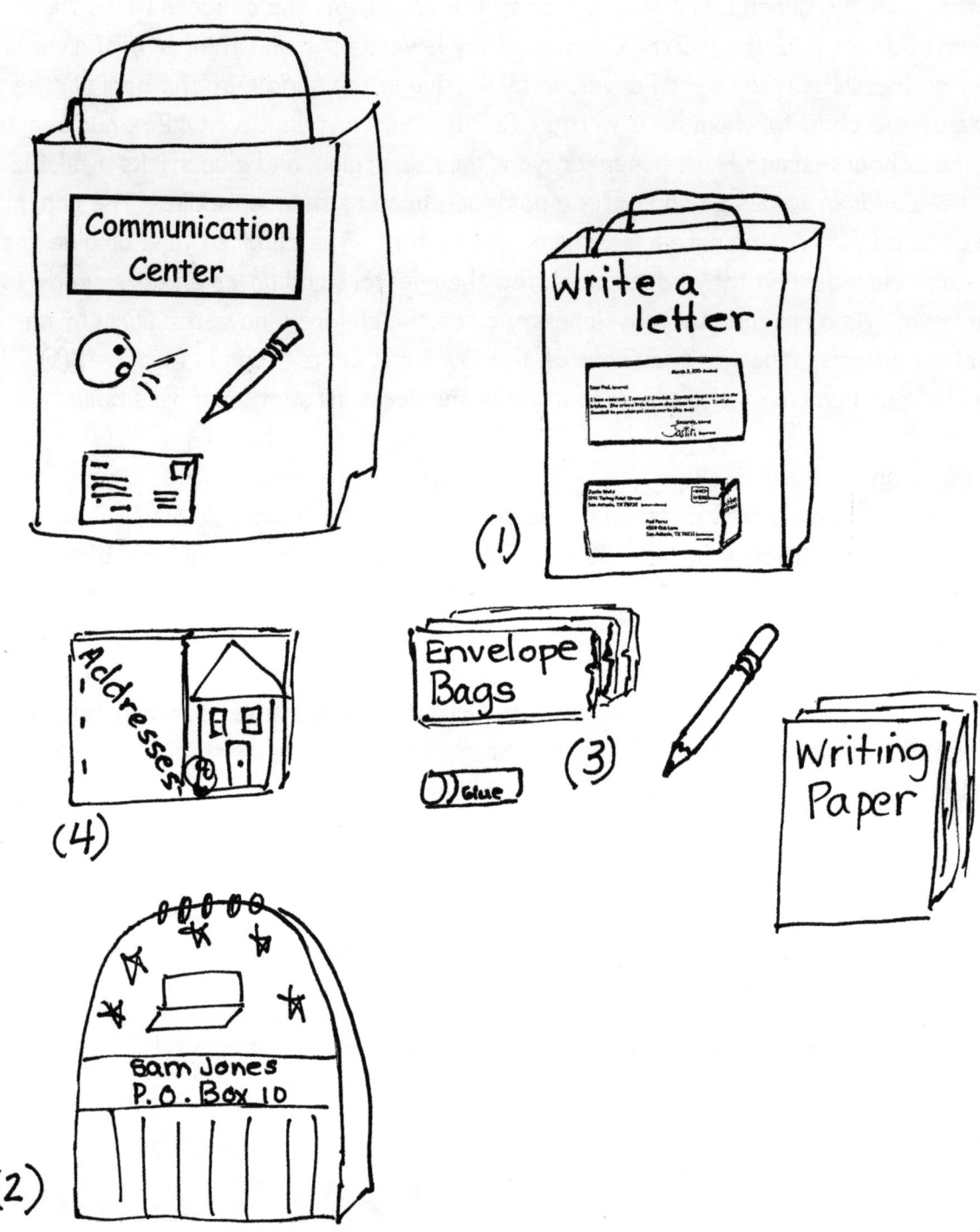

Figure 45

Make a Mailbox Bag

1. Cut the top of the bag in a curve.

2. Each child draws a mailbox design on his bag.

3. Each child chooses a Post Office Box Number and writes his name and the number ("P.O. Box XX") on the bag.

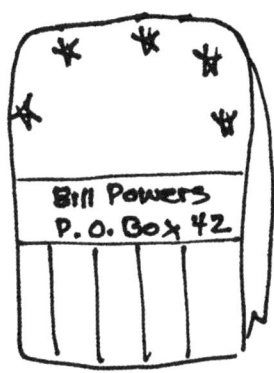

4. Open the bag; cut a mail slot flap in one side of the bag. Write "Mail Slot" on the flap (the flap extends outside the bag).

5. Paper clip the top of the bag closed.

Figure 46

8. Art Center

Here is a way to take up a small amount of space for an Art Center and, at the same time, reduce the mess usually associated with having an Art Center. The children will still have a good time.

Put the art activities in a large gift- or grocery bag. Label the front "Art Center." Use the following art activities. They can be removed from the bag by the children [please see Figure 47(1), (2), and (3)].

(1) <u>Hair Gel in a Baggie</u>
Use quart-size, resealable freezer *Baggies*. Add one-quarter cup of clear, hair gel, glitter, and foil stars. Close the bag slowly, releasing from the bag all the captured air. Smooth the mixture in the *Baggie*. When the mixture is smooth and all of the air has been released, reseal the bag and tape is closed with clear, plastic packing tape (so bag won't open accidentally). The children can draw designs in the gel through the side of the bag--smooth it out and do it again. No hands to wash!

(2) <u>Make a Rubbing of Objects in a Bag</u>
Use quart-size, resealable freezer *Baggies*. Affix flat objects to the inside back panel of the bag with *Sticky Tac*. Use a paper clip, a penny, a leaf, a foil star, and a feather. Spread the items out evenly on the inside back panel. Close the bag expelling all of the air, reseal and tape the over closure with clear plastic packing tape. The children make a rubbing of the objects in the bag. They use a crayon, with the paper peeled off, to rub over the objects in the *Baggie* until the objects' rubbings appear on the paper.

State standards that are met by using activities like (1) and (2):
    (1) Develops manipulative skills when drawing
    (2) Develops and organizes ideas by identifying colors, textures, forms and
        subjects in the environment
    (3) Creates artwork using a variety of media
    (4) Express ideas about personal artwork

(3) <u>Strip-Snipping Bag</u>
Put each child's name on a brown-paper lunch bag like: "Jason's Scissors Work." Cut one-inch-wide, colored construction-paper strips; store 10-12 strips in each bag. Start the children off by showing them how to use the scissors. Ask them to

practice by snipping the strips and putting them in the bag. As their skills evolve the bag will accumulate more snips to use to make a collage. For older children use wide strips. They can cut designs from their paper, rather than just snipping strips. You can add to this activity a study of the artist Henri Matisse. He used color cutouts and "scissor art" in the later periods of his work. The children can use their cuttings like Henri Matisse to make repeating, beautiful designs cut from paper.

State standards that are met by using activities like this one:
- (1) Develops pincher control
- (2) Learns to control the shoulder, arm, and hand movements to create
- (3) Develops fundamental physical skills and progresses from simple to more complex movements
- (4) Organizes disparate elements into artistic compositions
- (5) Applies art concepts

Figure 47

Loop-Stick Toy Tote

Bag Contents: Cardboard cylinder from a pant-hanger*, string, tape and one leg from a pair of "panty-hose-like", tights.

*Note: when pants are cleaned at the dry cleaners they are usually hung over a cardboard cylinder that connects each side of the pant hanger. If the cylinder is removed from the hanger is makes an excellent accessory for this and other activities.

1. Make a loop stick.

2. Use wire cutters to remove the hook from a wire hanger; bend the hanger as straight as possible. Cut it to 18-inches; use the wire cutters to fold an eye on one end. The wire should resemble a long needle with an eye on one end.

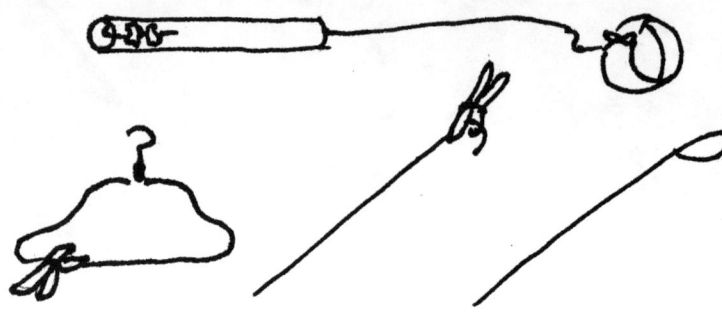

2. Thread the string through the needle eye; use the wire needle to push the string through the cardboard cylinder.

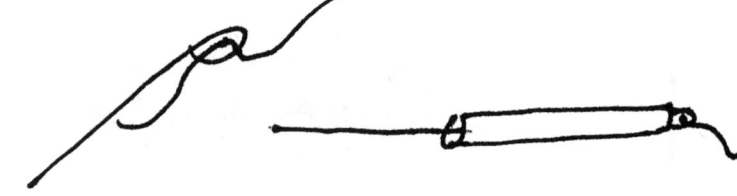

3. Fold one end of the string onto the cylinder tape it snuggly.

4. Cut off the foot of the tight. Slide the remaining tube up your arm to above the elbow, starting with the large end of the tight and working toward the ankle and then, roll it down to make a ring.

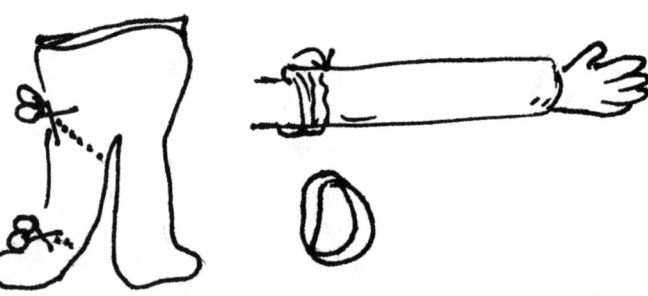

5. Tie the ring to the end of the string extending from the end of the cylinder.

6. Toss the ring with the stick and try to catch it on the end of the cylinder.

Telephone Toy-Tote

Bag Contents: two paper cups, two paper clips, and string.

1. Make a Telephone.

2. Use the pointed end of a pair of scissors to make a hole in the bottom of each of the two cups.

3. Thread the string through both the cup-bottom holes such that they meet bottom-to-bottom with the string extending out of the open end of both cups.

4. Tie a paperclip to each end of the string; pull the string until the clips resting against bottom of the inside of both cups.

5. Use the paper-cup "telephone" to talk to a family member or a friend.

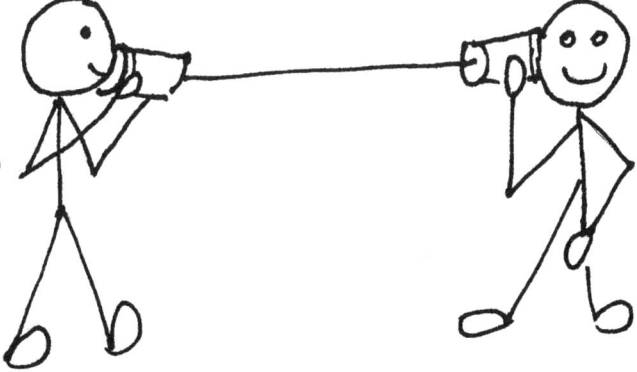

Picture-Puzzle Toy Tote

Bag Contents: A picture from a magazine, two sheets of construction paper, and a baggie.

1. Make a Picture Puzzle.

2. Cut the picture into as many pieces as your children can manage.

3. Glue the pieces to one of the sheets of construction paper; cut out the pieces again.

4. Make a puzzle base: Trace the pieces onto the second sheet of construction paper by putting all the pieces together in the solved-puzzle position and tracing around each silhouette. Store the puzzle pieces in the Baggie.

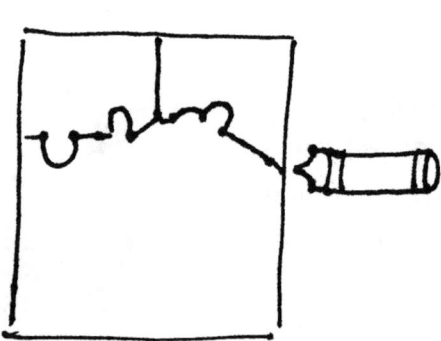

5. Work the puzzle!

Funnel-and-Container Toy Tote

Bag Contents: Plastic soda bottle (without a lid), sandpaper, and tape.

1. Make a funnel and container.

2. Cut the soda bottle in half.

3. Sand the container and funnel edges with the sand paper.

4. Tape a fill line on the container.

5. Let your child use the funnel for water play in the bath tub and with sand play.

Underwater Viewer Toy Tote

Bag Contents: A coffee can with a plastic lid, small sheet of clear-plastic wrap, and a rubber band.

1. Make an Underwater Viewer.

2. Remove the bottom of the can with a can opener.

3. Flatten the sharp and rough edges on the inside of the can with pliers.

4. Cover one end of the can with the clear-plastic wrap; hold the wrap in place with the rubber band and keep out the water.

5. Cut out the center of the plastic lid leaving about a half-inch border all around. Put the lid over the plastic wrap, on the end of the can, to hold the wrap in place.

6. Your child uses the viewer to look underwater in the bath tub, an aquarium, or a puddle of water.

Kazoo Toy Tote

Bag Contents: Cylinder, wax paper, construction paper, and a rubber band.

1. Make a kazoo.

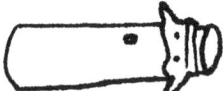

2. Cover the toilet paper cylinder with construction paper.

2. Make a hole in the cylinder with the pointed-end of a pair of scissors, about two inches from one end.

3. Cut the wax paper into a circle.

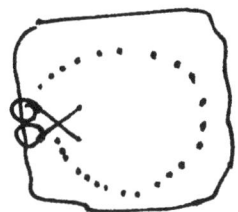

4. Cover the end near the hole with the wax-paper circle; hold it in place with the rubberband.

5. Have your child hum into the open end of the kazoo to make music.

Date:

Dear Parent(s):

You child will start off this school year reading what is called *environmental print*. It is the print from everyday life. Your child sees it everyday, as he comes to school in the car or on the bus.

Some examples of environmental print are on this page. It is familiar and friendly--rich with associations that each one of us has with it like, going out to a birthday dinner or buying a new pair of shoes to start school. Associations like these are helpful motivators in learning to read.

Our class will move to a formal reading program later in the school year. Reading environmental print is a good place for your child to begin what we hope will be a life-long love of reading. To help this along, please save labels to send to school to add to his or her reading bag. When you eat at your favorite store, or buy a favorite cereal or shoe, save the label and send it to school. The reading bag will hold all of the examples of environmental print your child has brought to school. We will read print from the bag everyday, so send some environmental print examples just as soon as your child hits on one of his or her interests.

Thank you for your help with this wonderful program.

Sincerely,

Your Child's Teacher

Story-Tag Bag Parent Letter

Date

Dear Parent,

This is your child's Story-Tag Bag. Inside the bag you will find a _____. It is a story tag; it is a reminder to your child of an experience he had with the story or an activity we did in association with the story. Your child knows this story well.

Encourage your child to tell the story to you or to a family member. This will help your child build a foundation for reading. Retelling a story, or an event, teaches your child the story sequence and how print is used to tell what happens. It also helps teach how sentences are structured with words in an order that conveys meaning. Your child also learns that stories have a beginning, middle and an end. All of this knowledge helps considerably when your child learns to read.

Your child will also practice voice inflexion, vocal tone, and facial expressions to help tell the story. Inflexion and expression gives stories life and gives your child added incentive to build vocabulary. When I find a story that is popular, or do something in school that is exciting, I will send home a story tag for you to add to the bag. It may be an item as simple as an apple-shaped eraser, but it will remind your child of a story experience; like when we make applesauce, for instance. Building experiences into stories helps your child retain thoughts, ideas, and events in the story.

Whenever your child reaches into his bag and pulls out a story tag, ask him to retell the story to you—with expression, if you please!

Sincerely,

Your Child's Teacher,

Toy Tote Letter to the Parents

Date

Dear Parent(s),

The brown paper bag I have sent home is full of materials to make a "Toy Tote." The directions are on the front of the bag. From time to time I will send home a Toy Tote; they are a fun way for you to make a toy with your child.

Each Toy Tote your child brings home helps build essential skills for his or her success in school, not only now, but also later on. For example, when your child "reads" the directions on the bag and tells you how to make the toy, he is beginning to read by using pictures. He is also learning to follow multi-step directions in numerical order. He will have to assemble the toy number-by-number for the toy to turn out right.

If you have the time, find a quiet spot at home and work together with your child. When you work, talk about the materials that go together to make the toy. Ask questions that invite him to explore the ways he thinks about the toy. For instance: "What is the same about the toy pieces?" "What is different?" "What colors do you see?" "How many pieces are here to make the toy?" If you were the toy, how would you be different?" "What do you like about the toy?" "Why?"

I know you and child will enjoy your toy making adventure.

Sincerely,

Your Child's Teacher

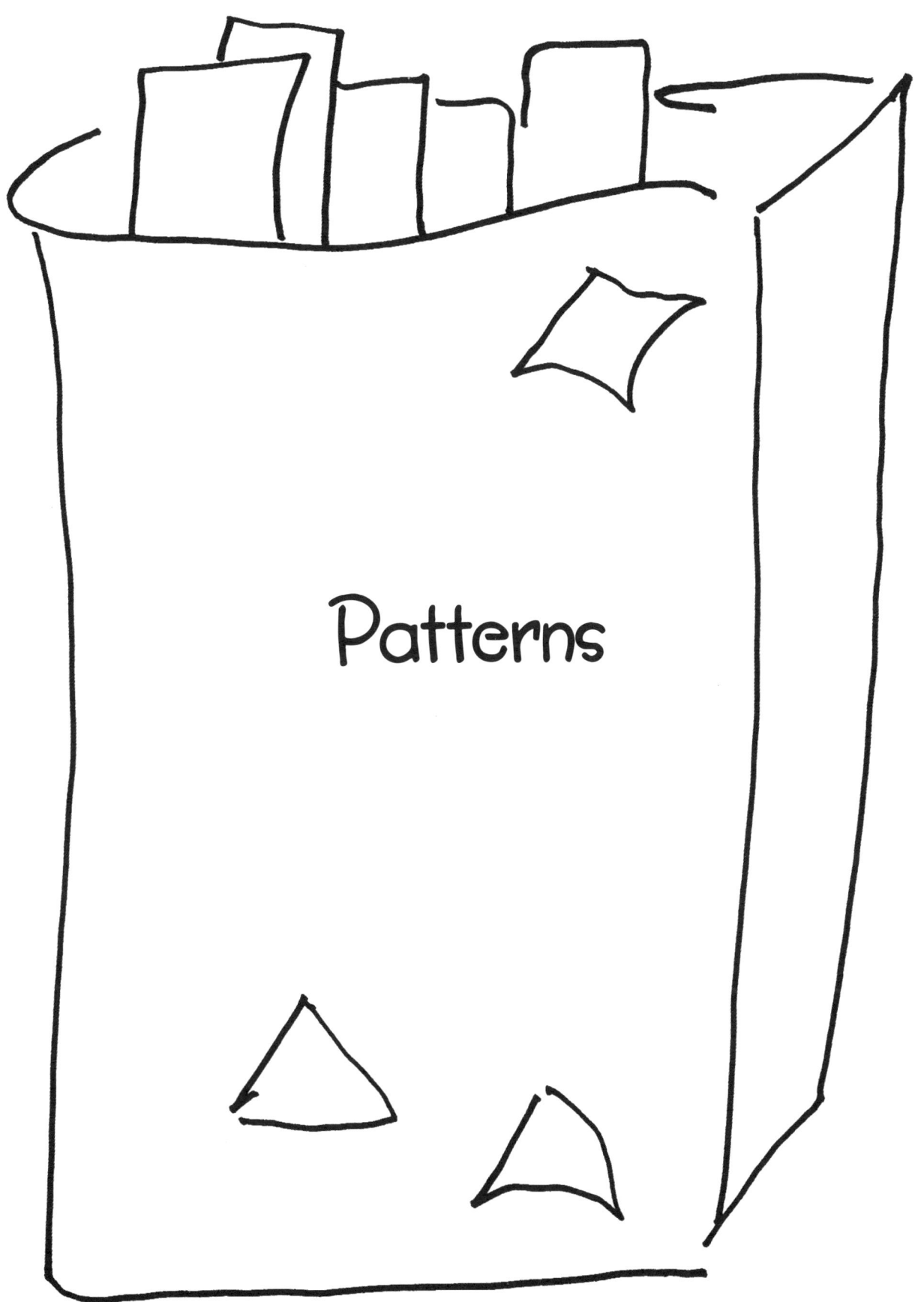

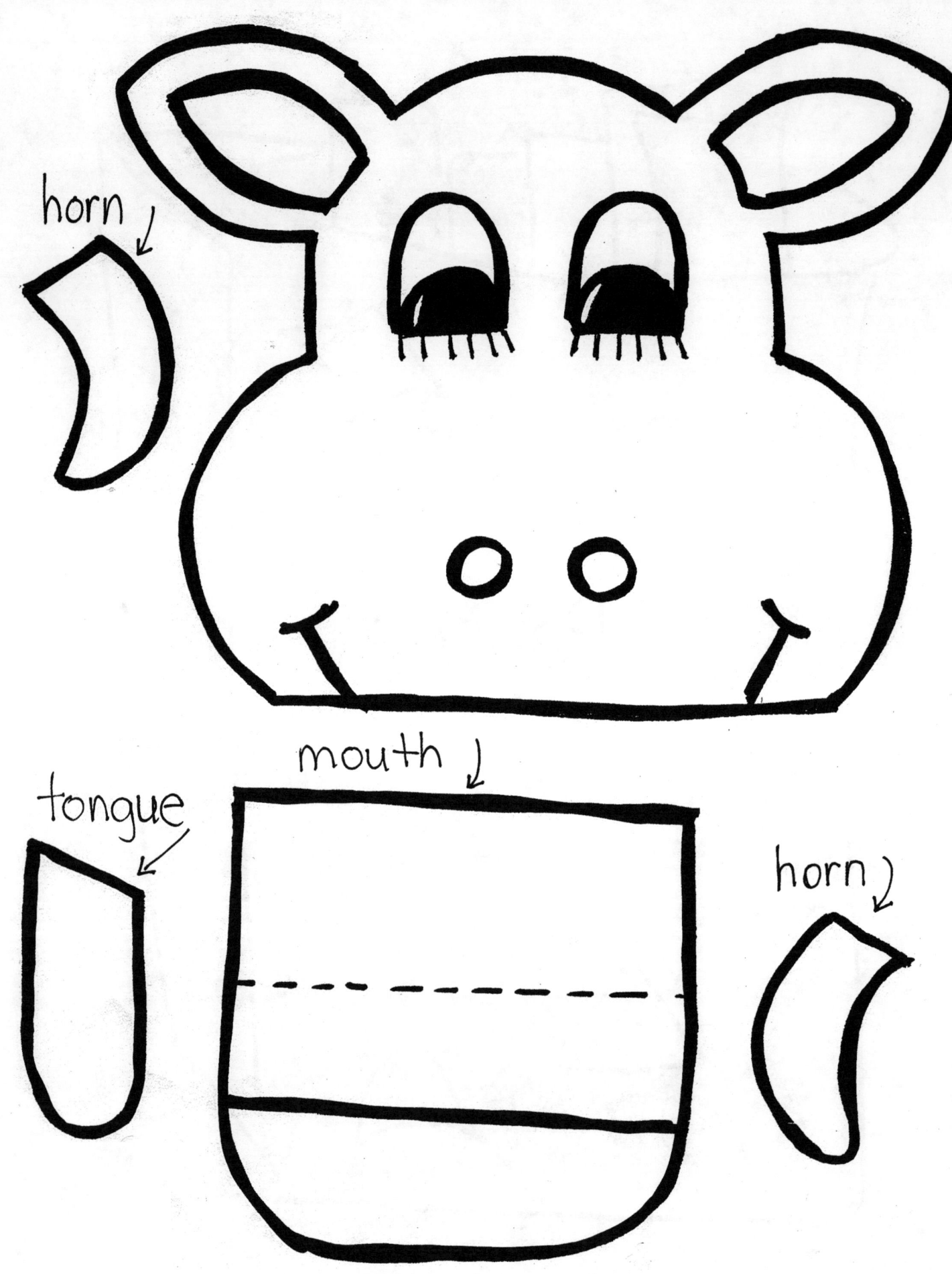

Tri Level Peanut Book Pictures

1. "Peanuts" picture.

2. "Seeds" picture.

3. "Peanut Butter" picture.

4. "Sandwich" picture.

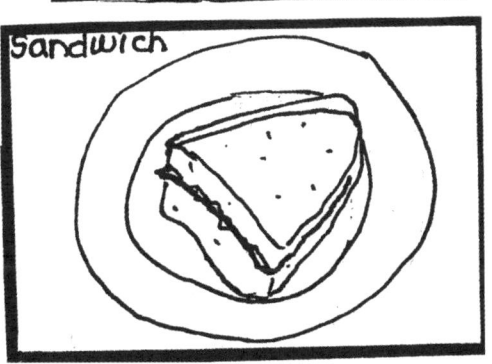

5. This is a "Jiff" label to use on the *baggie* that has the folded paper toweling in it to resemble peanut butter.

Pictures and Directions for Making the Butterfly Life Cycle Activity

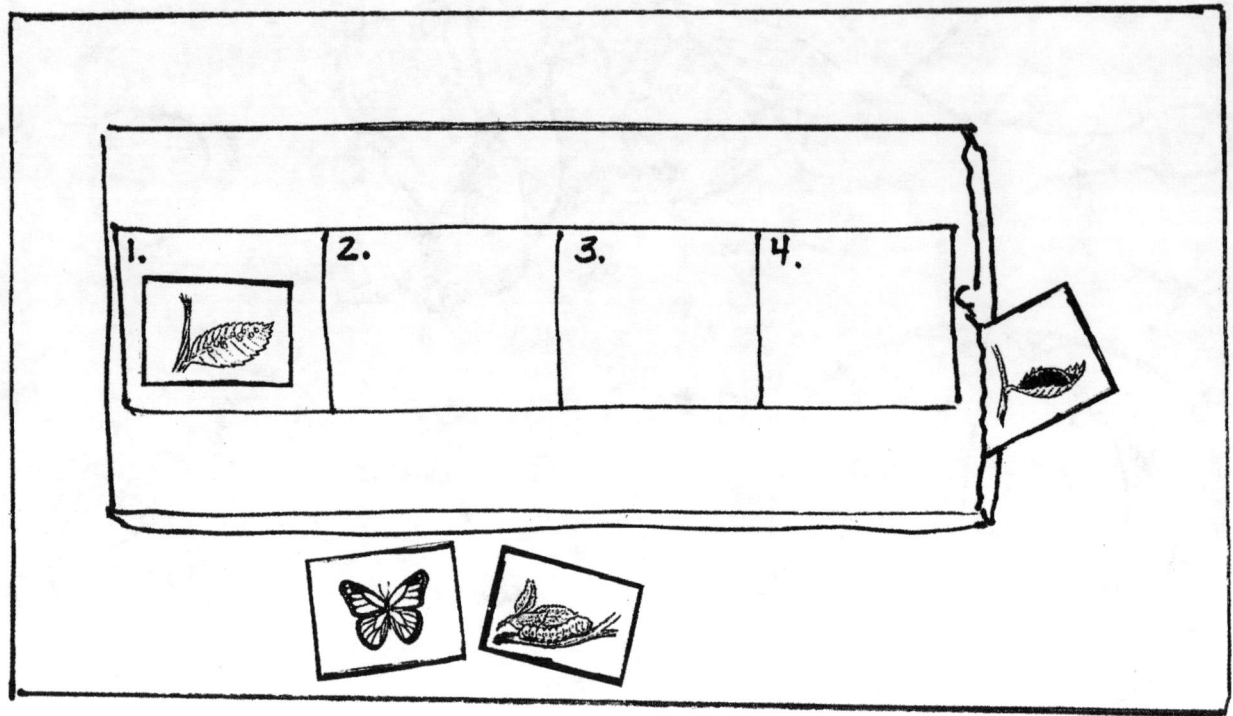

1. Cut out the picture directions above and back the page with construction paper.
2. Draw numbered boxes on the small lunch bag.
3. Color and cut out the sequence cards below. Back the cards with construction paper and cut them out again.
4. Laminate the picture directions, the bag, and the sequence cards. Store the pieces in the bag.

Woodworking Center

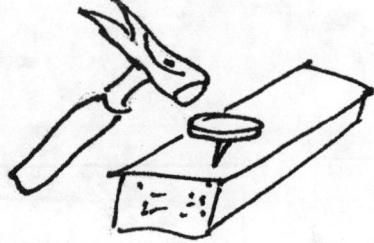

Creative Writing Center

Construction Center

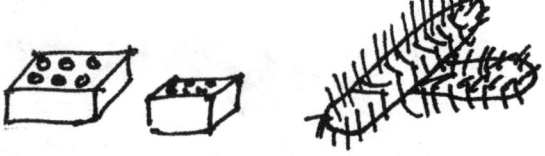

Pouring Table Center

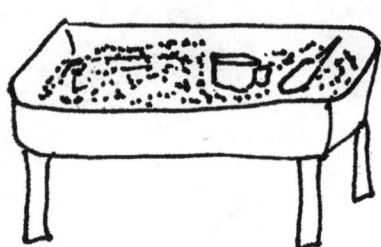

Play Dough Center

Outdoor Center

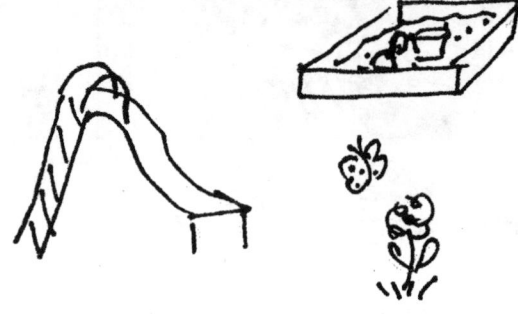

Story Telling Center

Overhead Center

Art Center

Games and Puzzles Center

Library Center

Computer Center

Science Center

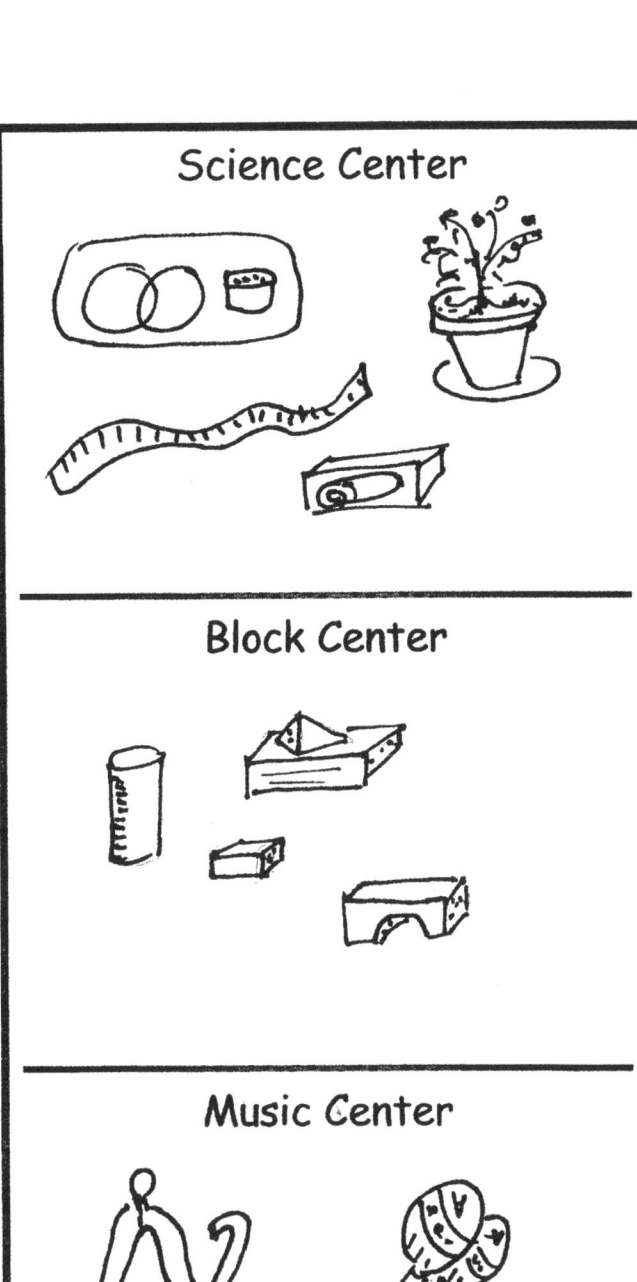

Block Center

Music Center

Home Living Center

Math Center

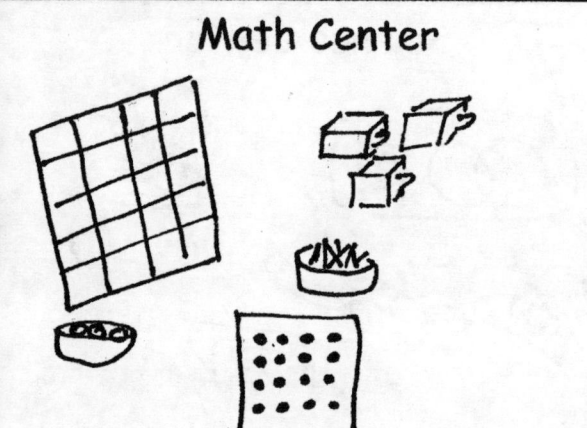

Geography Center

Handwriting Center

Listening Station

Spelling Center

Working with Words Center

Communication Center

Read the Room Center

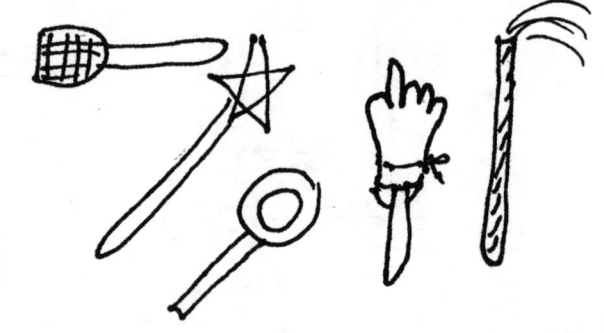

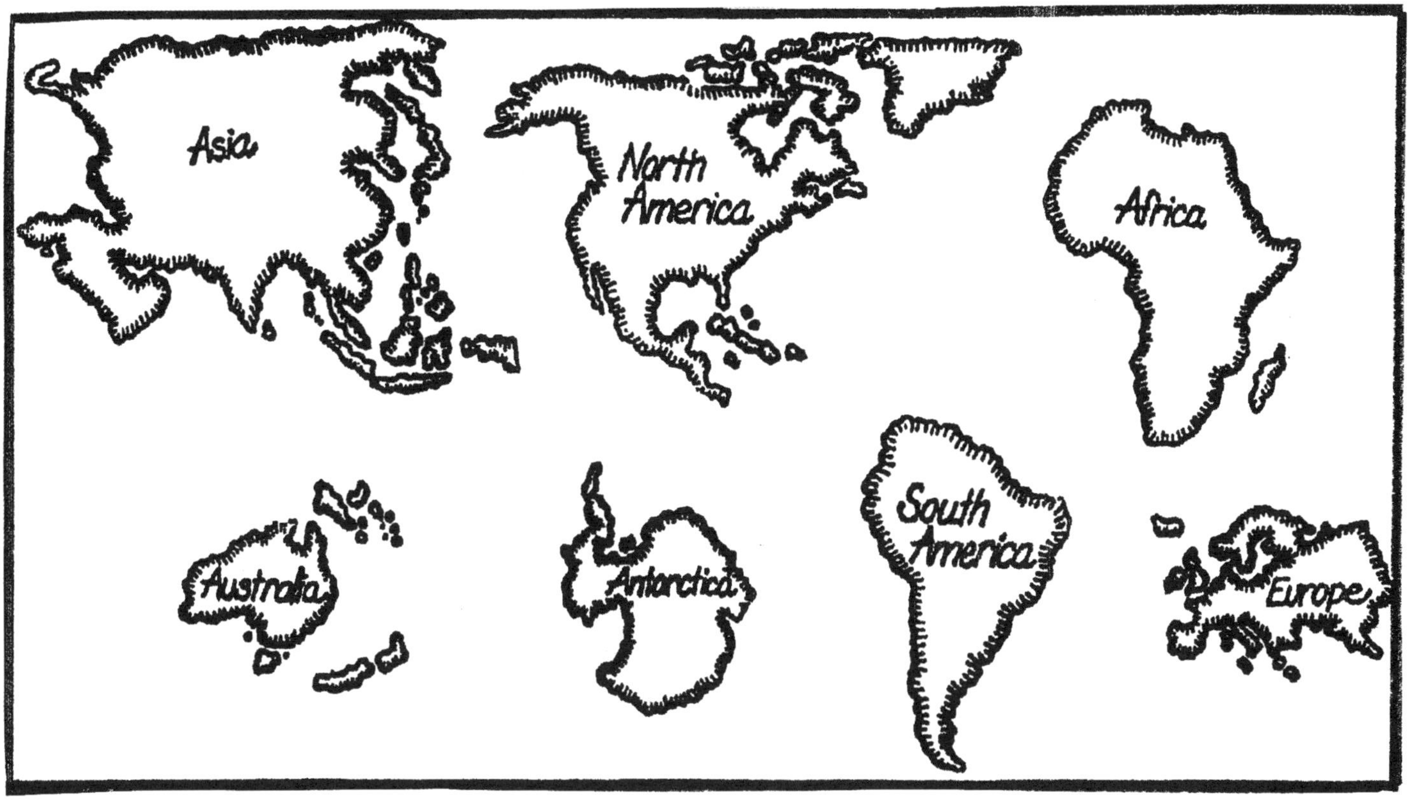
Asia
North America
Africa
South America
Australia
Antarctica
Europe

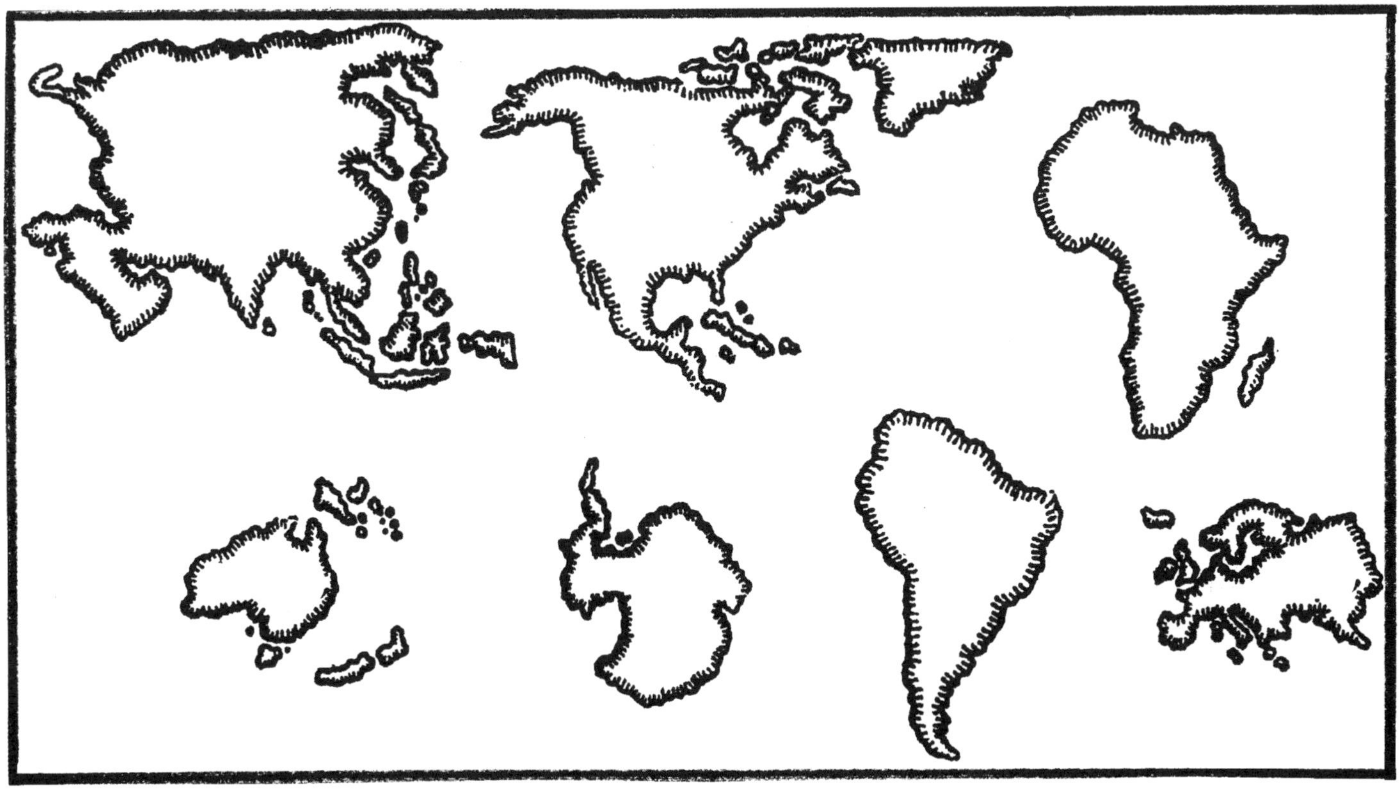

Venn Diagram

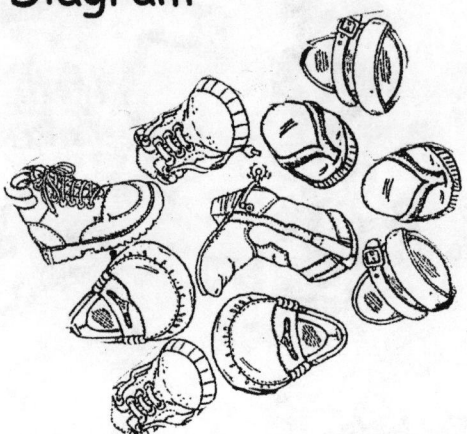

Take the items from the bag.

Examine the shoes and boots.

Find the shoes and boots that are for <u>Work</u>, <u>Play</u>, and <u>Work and Play.</u>

Place the shoes and boots for <u>Work</u> on the pink part of the diagram.

Place the shoes and boots for <u>Play</u> on the green part of the diagram.

Place the shoes and boots for <u>Work and Play</u> on the yellow part of the diagram.

Bean Drop Bag

Drop a few beans from the bag. Make a number sentence on the paper.

Write your number sentence.

2 + 3 = 5

Tally Directions

Get a sheet of paper.

Find the penny.

Flip the penny 12 times.

When it is heads put a tally mark.

When it is tails put a tally mark.

Write a letter to a friend. Remember to use the letter parts which include the *heading*, the *greeting*, the *body*, the *closing*, and the *signature*. Here is an example of a friendly letter.

March 3, 200- (heading)

Dear Paul, (greeting)

I have a new cat. I named it Snowball. Snowball sleeps in a box in the kitchen. She cries a little because she misses her Mama. I will show Snowball to you when you come over to play. (body)

Sincerely, (closing)
Justin (signature)

Here is an example of addressing an envelope. You put the person you are writing in the middle of the envelope. Write your return address in the upper left-hand corner and place the stamp in the upper right-hand corner.

Justin Wells
1241 Turkey Point Street
San Antonio, TX 78232   (return address)

(stamp)

Paul Perez
4509 Oak Lane
San Antonio, TX 78231 (person you are writing)